I0458429

# TESTIMONIALS

This book was given to me by Blake Watkins, at a very critical point of my career and life. During that challenging season, I could not see past the darkness that was surrounding me because I did not understand the authority God provides us in life. There are not enough words of gratitude for the wisdom found in this book. Goliath Code talks about the power of God and how He works through an individual who is full of faith. David understood the terrain of the battlefield he was approaching. He knew with God he would have ultimate victory despite the threats of Goliath. Often in today's society, we are not taught how to understand God's authority, and use God's authority to establish His kingdom. The Goliath Code provides powerful and important lessons that we can use in everyday life. I am profoundly grateful for this book and the friendship and mentoring that I've received through Blake Watkins.

- Robert S. Marsh, D.O., Board Certified and Fellowship Trained Orthopedic Surgeon, Advanced Orthopedics of Oklahoma

Well, I have found a book that I have thoroughly enjoyed reading several times… I have struggled for decades to find a single source, other than the Bible, to recommend to all new believers as they start their Christian walk - and now I have found it. The Goliath Code is a fresh look at how a believer can see themselves win in this battle of life by using the simple Biblical Principles covered in the book. It is organized in such a way that you can just read right through it if you want and devour the wealth of Biblical insights and references mixed with the author's personal applications. However, the book is much deeper on a closer look because the code the author explains is so practical that every believer needs to study and learn this code in their daily life.

Furthermore, there is a question-and-answer section in each chapter that can be used for personal or group Bible Study. So, the book can also be used as a guide by Pastors, teachers or just study groups to master who we are in Christ after they have been through it the first time. There is a particular focus from beginning to end on who we are in Christ and how we can slowly over time re-program our mind with Biblically-based truths. I cannot recommend this book enough for new believers, seasoned believers who want to help disciple others, and Pastors and teachers to implement this code in their churches. It is truly a Biblical Battle Plan.

- Gary Eubanks, Pastor, Retired

When my good friend, Blake Watkins, gifted to me his book, "The GOLIATH CODE," I remember being excited to read it simply because I knew the author personally. However, it didn't take long for me to appreciate what the book truly is: a well-researched, thoughtful, and inspirational perspective on the spiritual victory freely offered to us through faith in Jesus Christ. Blake does an excellent job of weaving the historical truth of one of the most well-known stories in human history – David vs Goliath – with the biblical truth of the victory claimed for Christians by Jesus. Using the acrostic GOLIATH CODE, Blake more than competently connects the theological insights of the incredible victory of David over Goliath with the spiritual armor, strength, and victory God has equally made available to us for our daily lives. I have personally benefited from what I've learned from Blake's insights, as have Bible study students that I have taught using "The GOLIATH CODE" as a commentary on Scripture. I highly recommend it for anyone who is looking for "a biblical battle plan" for living life biblically and victoriously.

– Lee Herring, Pastor, Broadway Baptist Church,
Sand Springs, Oklahoma

"The GOLIATH CODE is an exceptional resource for anyone seeking insight and inspiration on the subject of principled leadership in a culture that is defined by an appalling lack of it."

Manley Beasley Jr., Senior Pastor, Hot Springs Baptist Church,
Current President of the Arkansas Baptist State Convention

# THE
# GOLIATH
## CODE

## A BIBLICAL BATTLE PLAN
## FOR DEFEATING ANY GIANT

## BLAKE WATKINS

Copyright 2023 by Blake Watkins Goliath Code: A Biblical battleplan for Defeating Any Giant. All Rights Reserved

Published by Leadership Books, Inc. Las Vegas, NV – New York, NY LeadershipBooks.com

Previously published under ISBN 978-1-94670809-0 by Bold Vision Books, Friendswood, Texas 77549

ISBN: 978-1-965401-09-5 (Paperback)
ISBN: 978-1-965401-08-8 (Hardback)
ISBN: 978-1-965401-10-1 (eBook)

All Rights Reserved. No part of this publication may be reproduced, distributed, or transmitted in any form or by any means, including photocopying, recording, or other electronic or mechanical methods, without the prior written permission of the publisher, except in the case of brief quotations embodied in critical reviews and certain other noncommercial uses permit-ted by copyright law.

Leadership Books, Inc is committed to publishing works of quality and integrity. In that spirit, we are proud to offer this book to our readers; however, the story, the experiences, and the words are the authors alone. The conversations in the book all come from the author's recollections, not word-for-word transcripts. All of the events are true to the best of the author's memory. The author, in no way, represents any company, corporation, or brand mentioned herein. The views expressed are solely those of the author.

Unless otherwise noted Scripture quotations are taken from the New King James Version®. Copyright © 1982 by Tomas Nelson, Inc. Used by permission. All rights reserved.

Scripture quotations marked NASB are taken from the New American Standard Bible®, Copyright © 1960, 1962, 1963, 1968, 1971, 1972, 1973, 1975, 1977, 1995 by The Lockman Foundation. Used by permission. (www.Lockman.org)

**LEADERSHIP**
Thoughtful. Relevant Leaders From Around The World
BOOKS

# DEDICATION

To Jennie, my beautiful Proverbs 31 wife and best friend.

Your love, respect and encouragement continually remind me who I am in Christ. Your faith and faithfulness inspire everyone who knows you to walk closer to Jesus. Your promise to follow me wherever God leads us has held us together on this amazing life journey. I will forever be grateful to God for His grace in bringing you into my life and will always love you for staying.

To Wesley & Amber, Shannon & Matt, Jaiden & Brittany, Traiven, Caedmon, Amelia, Layne and Kaylee. I pray that you will be strong in the Lord and grasp who you are in Christ. Remember, the battle belongs to the Lord!

# TABLE OF CONTENTS

## PART III: THEY DID NOT LOVE THEIR
## LIVES UNTO DEATH

# ACKNOWLEDGMENTS

Writing a book for publication is a more complicated endeavor than I ever imagined. I could never have endured without the support and encouragement of all my family, friends and students. Thank you, all.

Thank you, Jennie Watkins, for encouraging me to stick with it when I suffered the dreaded writer's block; and for giving me flexibility with my honey-do list to spend time writing.

Thank you, Shannon Watkins (my daughter and webmaster), for helping me with early manuscript edits and for creating and maintaining my online presence. Thank you, Jim and Carolyn Watkins (my mom and dad), for your prayers, guidance and godly example. Thank you, Wesley and Amber Watkins (my son and daughter-in-law) and Jaiden and Traiven Altom (my grandsons), for your encouragement. Thank you, Caedmon and Layne Altom and Amelia and Kaylee Watkins (my youngest grandkids), for your love and joy.

Thank you, Dr. Rodney Reeves and Pastor Stephen Spurgin, for demonstrating and instilling in me a deep love and respect for the written Word of God.

Thank you, John 3:16 Ministries, for the experience and opportunity of a lifetime.

"And they overcame him by the blood of the Lamb,

and by the word of their testimony,

and they did not love their lives to the death."

(Revelation 12:1)

# PROLOGUE

The most famous battle of all time occurred over three thousand years ago, yet we still tell its story to our children and grandchildren.

We describe the soldiers. We explain the weapons and even how much ammunition was used. The names of the main characters—David and Goliath—are interwoven into our culture.

Because it is also our story, it applies to each of us.

We each fight spiritual battles like this one, facing enemies bigger, stronger, and more experienced than us. We have adversaries who seem like giants—giants who hate us and try to stop us from doing what God has created, called and empowered us to do. These giants want to drag us back into bondage and destroy us.

This saga is an example of amazing bravery and courage in the face of shameful cowardice, fear, arrogant pride, and impossible odds. It is a story perfect for the big screen, but there is more. Beneath the surface of this familiar story is a "secret code" of vital information we can use to win our battles with the giants who come against us. I call it *The Goliath Code.*

> "It is the glory of God to conceal a matter, but the glory of kings is to search out a matter" (Proverbs 25:2).

The foundation of *The Goliath Code* is an unshakable faith in the absolute truth of God's Word, the Bible. Stories like this one are not mere allegory or mythology. Skeptics try to use such stories as "proofs" the Bible cannot be taken as real history, much less inerrant.

But I stand on what Jesus said to the Father in the garden:

"Your Word is truth" (John 17:17).

And as the Psalmist said:

"The entirety of Your Word is truth ..." (Psalm 119:105).

I agree with Augustine when he said, "If you believe what you like in the Bible, and don't believe what you don't like in the Bible, then it is not the Bible you believe—it is yourself." We must let the Bible judge us, rather than us judge it.

"For the Word of God is living and powerful, and sharper than any two-edged sword, piercing even to the division of soul and spirit, and of joints and marrow, and is a discerner of the thoughts and intents of the heart" (Hebrews 4:12).

David's victory vividly illustrates how we, too, can conquer our giants. I created the acrostic GOLIATH CODE to help you remember and apply this biblical strategy to your spiritual battles.

Each letter in this mnemonic corresponds to a key word that heads each chapter and summarizes the main theme of the part of the battle plan contained in the passage.

To help you grasp the truths embedded in this story, I have divided each chapter into two parts—History and Strategy. The History sections focus on the Scripture narrative and its context. The Strategy sections illustrate how we can apply these truths to the battles we face today. After these two parts, I provide you with some questions to get your journey started.

My prayer is that you, if you are a child of the King, will glory in the search for the amazing truths concealed in this story and that you will allow God's Word to pierce into you, pruning your thoughts and beliefs.

Finally, if you have not yet decided to accept Jesus as your Lord, then I pray you will meet Him through this book and choose to place your trust in Him. Then—and only then—you, like David, can run to the battle in confidence and be more than a conqueror through Him who loves us.

~Blake Watkins

# Part I

# THE BLOOD OF THE LAMB

# The GOLIATH CODE

G:    Geography—Understand the Geography

O:    Opponent—Recognize Your Opponent

L:    Labels—Use the Right Labels

I:    Intrepid—Be Intrepid

A:    Aim—Aim to Please God

T:    Truth—Speak the Truth

H:    Hardware—Use the Right Hardware

C:    Confess—Confess the Lord

O:    Overcome—Overcome!

D:    Demonstrate—Demonstrate Your Faith

E:    Endure—Endure to the End

# Chapter One

# GEOGRAPHY

## HISTORY: THE BATTLEFIELD

"Now the Philistines gathered their armies together to battle, and were gathered at Sochoh, which belongs to Judah; they encamped between Sochoh and Azekah, in Ephes Dammim. And Saul and the men of Israel were gathered together, and they encamped in the Valley of Elah, and drew up in battle array against the Philistines. The Philistines stood on a mountain on one side, and Israel stood on a mountain on the other side, with a valley between them" (1 Samuel 17:1-3).

This was the Promised Land of Canaan that God gave to Abraham's descendants forever. In Joshua's day, it was a beautiful, well-watered and fruitful land, "flowing with milk and honey" (Numbers 13:27).

Before God led Israel across the Jordan River to enter the Promised Land from the East, a technologically-advanced tribe of warriors migrated across the Mediterranean Sea and invaded from the

West. These Philistines (whose name means "rolling" or "migrating") began their colonization of the land of Canaan around 2000 BC, during the time of Abraham. No one is certain where they came from, although there are several intriguing theories. Perhaps they were colonists from one of the ancient Greek city-states. One legend says they were survivors of the Trojan War.

Wherever they came from, their numbers and strength increased until they became Israel's most stubborn opponent and the most formidable obstacle blocking Israel from settling in the Promised Land.

The epic battle between David and Goliath began with a Philistine invasion into the territory of Judah. They marched across the border and set up camp between two tiny towns named Azekah and Sochoh. Azekah was on the edge of Philistine territory, in the coastal plain at the foot of the Judean hills. Sochoh, an Israeli hill town, was located on the western frontier of Judah, and marked the furthest point Israel had progressed in their conquest of the Promised Land.

I wonder whether the inhabitants understood the spiritual significance of their seemingly insignificant little villages. What could possibly be noteworthy about these tiny settlements?

It was their biblical names, which are often profoundly descriptive. Bible names were carefully chosen—not flippantly assigned. Even in America, place names often have significant meanings.

On a bank of the White River in north Arkansas, not far from my hometown, there is a small town named Oil Trough. Local historians say that, in the early 1800s, the fields and woods around there were teeming with bears. Bear hunting was a lucrative industry, providing meat, fur, and most importantly oil and grease. People used bear oil for cooking, lighting and lubrication. Apparently, there was a sizable rendering facility at Oil Trough, with large vats (or troughs) for storing the oil and shipping it downriver to the Mississippi. Hence the name: Oil Trough.

Just a few miles to the north lies the town of Cave City. With a population of less than two thousand people, the founders were overly optimistic in calling it a city. But it sits right over a large cave, which brings a little tourism to the local economy.

A bigger town nearby on the White River is Newport. There was once a booming river port just around the bend from Newport, in the heyday of commercial steamboat shipping. However, when the railroad came through, thanks to local politics, the railroad barons simply bypassed the old port town and built a new port to connect the railroad to the river traffic. The old port town faded away and all its businesses moved to Newport.

I recently lived in Texarkana, Texas, where the Arkansas-Texas border runs through the middle of downtown, right under the US Post Office. The city's name is derived from TEXas, ARKansas, and LouisiANA. One of the earliest songs I remember from my childhood is "Cotton Fields." I don't remember who sang it, although several famous artists have recorded it. One line of the song says, "It was down in Louisiana, just about a mile from Texarkana, in them old cotton fields back home." I grew up believing that Texarkana was on the border of Texas, Arkansas, and Louisiana, but was disappointed to learn that Louisiana is thirty miles from Texarkana!

So, you can see that American names are often meaningful and Hebrew names are much more so. Biblical names evoke history, assuredly, but are also prophetic—and inspired by God. That is the case with the Hebrew words *Azekah* and *Sochoh*, as well as most of the other names in this text.

In Hebrew, *Azekah* literally means "fence" and *Sochoh* means "hedge." Hedges and fences were made for protection against invasion, as seen in one of Jesus' parables:

> "There was a certain landowner who planted a vineyard and set a hedge around it, dug a winepress in it and built a tower" (Matthew 21:33).

Satan claimed God was protecting Job with a spiritual hedge.

> "Have You not made a hedge around him, around his household, and around all that he has on every side?" (Job 1:10).

And in Psalm 139, David praises God for His protection.

> "You have hedged me behind and before, and laid Your hand upon me" (Psalm 139:5).

I doubt the Philistines realized they were spiritually hemmed in between a hedge and a fence! But that's not all. The no-man's land on the border between the Philistines and the Israelites was called *Ephes Dammim*.

That word is one of those hard-to-pronounce names we often skip over when reading the Bible. But God never wastes words. Hidden in this name is a treasure far more precious than silver and gold (see 1 Peter 1:18).

The Hebrew name *Ephes Dammim* translates into English as "the boundary of the blood drops."

*Selah. Selah* means "Stop and think about this." Or, as my friend Michael would say, "Whoa!"

What were the early Israelites referring to when they named this area? According to Joshua chapter 10, this is the same region where the sun miraculously stood still in the sky for a whole day. There the Lord cast giant hailstones down from heaven and defeated the Amorites. Perhaps the name recalls that bloody battle.

Or maybe the name reminded the Israelites of the night before their ancestors left Egypt. They were safe from the horrors of the Passover night because of the blood on their doors, which the angel of death could not cross.

> "When He [the Lord] sees the blood on the lintel and on the two doorposts, the Lord will pass over the door and not allow the destroyer to come into your houses to strike you" (Exodus 12:23).

In either case, the Israelite army apparently didn't take much comfort from the name *Ephes Dammim* when the Philistines invaded.

Can you see it? The enemy forces blocked God's people from finishing what God had told them to do, which was to occupy all the land of Canaan. Then they tried to attack them and take back what God had given to His people. Without realizing it, they were supernaturally constrained between a hedge and a fence—stopped at the boundary of the blood!

Contrast the Philistines' position with the Israelites'. God's army, led by King Saul, camped in a place called *Elah*, beside the dry riverbed (or wadi), also called *Elah*, which is an amazing word. It is usually translated "oak," but its root is *"El,"* the most common Hebrew name for God. Somewhat like a strong oak, *El* can mean "ram" or "strength." Think of an oak battering ram or the phrase "Ram Tough."

The "ah" suffix is the Hebrew letter *Hey*. This is the same letter God added to Abram's name to change it to Abraham, and to Sarai's to make Sarah. The letter *Hey* is the Hebrew number five, which is the number for grace. So *Elah* refers to the grace of God. And *Elah* is the Aramaic name for God, found several times in the books of Ezra and Daniel. *Elah* is closely related to, if not the same as, the word *"Eloi"* that Jesus used on the cross when He cried out, "My God, my God, why have You forsaken me?"

By grace, the Israelites had arrayed in the position of strength, in God Himself, who is our strength. But they didn't comprehend that; at least, they did not acknowledge it.

# STRATEGY: UNDERSTAND THE GEOGRAPHY

Our enemies cannot stop us from doing what God created and called us to do—unless we let them. The key word Geography indicates the first step in learning how not to let them. First, we must understand the geography of the battlefield.

According to the Bible, Satan is our enemy. He hates us because he hates God who created and loves us. His hatred is rooted in his pride and envy of the Most High God. He fancies himself as greater than God. God describes Satan's arrogance in Isaiah, where he says:

> "I will ascend into heaven, I will exalt my throne above the stars of God; I will also sit on the mount of the congregation on the farthest sides of the north; I will ascend above the heights of the clouds, I will be like the Most High" (Isaiah 14:13-14).

The Hebrew word for God here is *El* and the word for Most High is *"Elyon."*

Because of Satan's pride, he rebelled against God. Therefore, God cast him down from his original lofty position as one of the most beautiful of God's creatures. I believe God portrayed this event in this mysterious passage in Ezekiel,

> "Therefore, I cast you as a profane thing out of the mountain of God; and I destroyed you, O covering cherub, from the midst of the fiery stones. Your heart was lifted up because of

your beauty; you corrupted your wisdom for the sake of your splendor; I cast you to the ground" (Ezekiel 28:16b-17).

Since Satan can't touch *Elyon*, he terrorizes those He loves and vents his anger on us. His first recorded act of rebellion was when he appeared as a serpent and successfully tempted Eve, and thereby Adam, to sin against God.

He also convinced one-third of the angels to join him in the rebellion, as depicted in Revelation 12.

> "And another sign appeared in heaven: behold a great, fiery red dragon having seven heads and ten horns, and seven diadems on his heads. His tail drew a third of the stars of heaven and threw them to the earth" (Revelation 12:3-4a).

> "And war broke out in heaven: Michael and his angels fought with the dragon; and the dragon and his angels fought, but they did not prevail nor was a place found for them in heaven any longer. So the great dragon was cast out, that serpent of old, called the Devil and Satan, who deceives the whole world; he was cast to the earth, and his angels were cast out with him" (Revelation 12:7-9).

Now his demonic force of fallen angels comes against us to block us from doing what God created us to do.

> "Woe to the inhabitants of the earth and the sea! For the devil has come down to you, having great wrath, because he knows that he has a short time" (Revelation 12:12).

"Be sober, be vigilant; because your adversary the devil walks about like a roaring lion, seeking whom he may devour. Resist him, steadfast in the faith, knowing that the same sufferings are experienced by your brotherhood in the world" (1 Peter 5:8-9).

"Yes, and all who desire to live godly in Christ Jesus will suffer persecution" (2 Timothy 3:12).

Nevertheless, as soldiers in the Lord's army and in His protection, we hold the position of strength—our adversaries do not.

"And I give them eternal life, and they shall never perish; neither shall anyone snatch them out of My hand. My Father, who has given them to Me, is greater than all; and no one is able to snatch them out of My Father's hand" (John 10:28-29).

And the spiritual hedge of protection God has placed in their path restricts their movement.

Can the enemy reach us who are in Christ? Not without crossing the boundary of "the precious blood of Christ, a lamb without blemish or defect" (1 Peter 1:19).

"To Him who loved us and washed us from our sins in His own blood, and has made us kings and priests to His God and Father, to Him be glory and dominion forever and ever. Amen" (Revelation 1:5-6).

Never forget where you are. If you are a Christian, the Bible says you are "in Christ." The New Testament uses the phrase more than eighty-five times, and it is the most common description of those who are saved (compared to only three instances for the word Christian).

For instance:

"… the gift of God is eternal life in Christ Jesus our Lord" (Romans 6:23b).

"There is therefore now no condemnation to those who are in Christ Jesus …" (Romans 8:1).

"As in Adam all die, even so in Christ all shall be made alive" (1 Corinthians 15:22).

"For all the promises of God in Him are Yes, and in Him Amen, to the glory of God through us" (2 Corinthians 1:20).

"Now thanks be to God who always leads us in triumph in Christ!" (2 Corinthians 2:14).

"If anyone is in Christ, he is a new creation …" (2 Corinthians 5:17).

"For we are His workmanship, created in Christ Jesus for good works, which God prepared beforehand that we should walk in them" (Ephesians 2:10).

"… be strong in the grace that is in Christ Jesus" (2 Timothy 2:1).

"Peace to you all who are in Christ Jesus. Amen" (1 Peter 5:14).

In the Old Testament, forgiveness for sins required the sacrifice of a perfect ram without any blemish, as in Leviticus 6 and elsewhere. Christ's substitutionary atonement was foreshadowed in Genesis by the ram caught in the thicket when Abraham was about to offer Isaac. John the Baptist declared Jesus to be the Lamb of God who takes away the sin of the world. A male lamb is called a ram. So, if we are in Christ, then we are in "the ram."

Less than a year after we moved to Oklahoma, an EF5 tornado devastated the city of Moore, a suburb of Oklahoma City. I was at work, watching through a window, mesmerized by the storm to the south. My wife was at home in the closet under the stairs, watching the storm online and listening to the TV. My daughter and three grandsons were huddled in their hallway in Midwest City, about eight miles northeast of Moore, and directly in the line of the storm. Everyone was praying.

The meteorologists warned those in the storm's path that the only way to survive was to be in a shelter.

Thankfully, while the world was watching live, the powerful 1.3-mile-wide tornado dissipated like smoke into the clouds—missing Midwest City by about three miles.

Sometime afterwards, we saw one of the above-ground, home storm shelters that had survived the Moore tornado. The 210-mph wind had sand-blasted most of the paint off the slightly dented, heavy-gauge-steel walls. But it was intact and had saved the lives of the family inside when the house around it disintegrated. They survived, unharmed, because they were in the shelter.

Christ is our shelter. To be in Christ is to be secure inside an indestructible shelter.

> "For You have been a shelter for me, a strong tower from the enemy" (Psalm 61:3).

> "Deliver me, O Lord, from my enemies; in You I take shelter" (Psalm 143:9).

Can the enemy harm us who are in Christ? Only if God, in His perfect wisdom and love, allows it. Satan had to ask permission to harm Job and his family (see Job 1:11-12; 2:5-6.) The devil had to ask Jesus before he could get to Peter.

> "And the Lord said, 'Simon, Simon! Indeed, Satan has asked for you, that he may sift you as wheat. But I have prayed for you, that your faith should not fail; and when you have returned to Me, strengthen the brethren'" (Luke 22:31-32).

But, if God decides to allow our enemies to touch us, can they kill us? Only our flesh.

> "And do not fear those who kill the body but cannot kill the soul. But rather fear Him who is able to destroy both soul and body in Hell. Are not two sparrows sold for a copper coin? And not one of them falls to the ground apart from your Father's will. But the very hairs of your head are all numbered. Do not fear therefore; you are of more value than many sparrows" (Matthew 10:28-31).

> "… I will build my church, and the gates of Hell shall not prevail against it" (Matthew 16:18).

# THE GOLIATH CODE

G:    Geography—Understand the Geography

O:    Opponent—Recognize Your Opponent

L:    Labels—Use the Right Labels

I:    Intrepid—Be Intrepid

A:    Aim—Aim to Please God

T:    Truth—Speak the Truth

H:    Hardware—Use the Right Hardware

C:    Confess—Confess the Lord

O:    Overcome—Overcome!

D:    Demonstrate—Demonstrate Your Faith

E:    Endure—Endure to the End

# THINK ABOUT IT—TALK ABOUT IT

### G: Understand the Geography

Are you "in Christ"? If you cannot confidently say, "yes", then, the strategy in The Goliath Code will not work for you. But you can be, so please stop right here and turn to "Annex 1: The ABCs of Salvation," located towards the end of this book—read God's free offer.

What do you think it means to be "in Christ"?

_____

_____

How does knowing you are in Christ affect your confidence level?

_____

_____

How is Christ like a storm shelter?

_____

_____

Since our enemy is spiritually hemmed in, can he hurt us?

_____

_____

Why do you think the Israelites did not understand the significance of the battlefield geography?

_____

_____

# Chapter Two

# OPPONENT

## HISTORY: THE ADVERSARY

"And a champion went out from the camp of the Philistines, named Goliath, from Gath, whose height was six cubits and a span. He had a bronze helmet on his head, and he was armed with a coat of mail, and the weight of the coat was five thousand shekels of bronze. And he had bronze armor on his legs and a bronze javelin between his shoulders. Now the staff of his spear was like a weaver's beam, and his iron spearhead weighed six hundred shekels; and a shield bearer went before him.

Then he stood and cried out to the armies of Israel, and said to them, 'Why have you come out to line up for battle? Am I not a Philistine, and you the servants of Saul? Choose a man for yourselves, and let him come down to me. If he is able to fight with me and kill me, then we will be your servants. But if I prevail against him and kill him, then you shall be our servants and serve us.' And the Philistine said, 'I defy the armies of Israel this day; give me a man, that we may fight together.' When Saul and all Israel heard these words of the Philistine, they were dismayed and greatly afraid" (1 Samuel 17:4-11).

The name Goliath has become synonymous with the word "giant." At nine feet nine inches tall, he certainly qualified as a giant, even though the Bible does not specifically use that term for him. However, the Bible does say (in 2 Samuel 21 and 1 Chronicles 20) that his father was a giant. The Hebrew word for "giant" in those two passages is *rapha,* which actually means super-strong. Elsewhere, such as in Genesis 6, the word for giant is *nephil,* which means feller. But not the kind of "feller" Ellie Mae Clampett was looking for! A feller is someone who causes things—or people—to fall. Another word which is sometimes translated as "giant" is *gibbor,* which means powerful bully or tyrant. The Greek language version of the Old Testament, known as the *Septuagint,* commonly renders these words as *gigantes,* from which we get our English words "gigantic" and "giant." Based on the depiction in 1 Samuel, Goliath was indeed a gigantic, super-strong, powerful bully of a feller.

But did giants ever exist? Really? In Genesis, the Bible declares there were giants in the days before the flood and afterward in the days of Moses.

"There were giants on the earth in those days, and also afterward, when the sons of God (Elohim) came in to the daughters of men (Adam) and they bore children to them.

These were the mighty men of old, men of renown" (Genesis 6:4).

The Hebrew word for them here is *Nephilim,* which is the plural form of *nephil,* and is most often translated "fallen," as in:

"How you are fallen from heaven, O Lucifer, son of the morning! How you are cut down to the ground, you who weakened the nations!" (Isaiah 14:12)

The *Nephilim* were the offspring of the "sons of *Elohim*" and the "daughters of Adam." Elsewhere in the Old Testament, such as in the Book of Job, the phrase "sons of *Elohim (God)*" refers to angels. The oldest and most common understanding of this passage is that fallen angels somehow caused human women to give birth to giants.

The Bible does not explain how this could happen—only that it did. Angels do not normally have physical bodies, though they can temporarily assume human form (see Genesis 18). Furthermore, in Matthew 22:30, Jesus affirmed they do not marry, at least not anymore.

Nevertheless, they could have possessed the women or their mates. Possession often involves drug use and drug use often leads to birth defects. The Greek word for "sorcery" in the New Testament is *pharmakia,* from which we get the English words "pharmacy" and "pharmaceutical." Sorcery, demonic possession, and illicit drug use go hand-in-hand. A born-again, former meth cook once told me that the best cooks had secret recipes which they would chant aloud when preparing batches of crystal meth. He had no doubt that the formulas were actually demonic incantations.

Another possible explanation is cloning or genetic manipulation. That may sound incredible but remember that people lived an average of 930 years before the flood. How smart would we be today if we all lived that long? We don't know how far technology had advanced before the world perished in the flood. (We still don't know how they were able to build the pyramids.)

Solomon said:

> "That which has been is what will be, that which is done is what will be done, and there is nothing new under the sun. Is there anything of which it may be said, "See, this is new"? It has already been in ancient times before us. There is no remembrance of former things, nor will there be any remembrance of things that are to come by those who will come after" (Ecclesiastes 1:9-11).

Nowadays, human cloning is a satanic-inspired attempt by men to play God. Why not back then? After all, Satan keeps using the same tactics over and over in his dealings with humans, and we keep falling for his schemes.

These *Nephilim* crossbreeds between "gods" and humans are main characters in the histories of numerous cultures. For instance, Greek mythology speaks of the demigods such as Hercules, Achilles, Perseus, and even the beautiful Helen of Troy.

Wherever they came from, the original Nephilim all drowned in the flood. However, somehow, there were more of them by the time the Israelites first spied out the Promised Land.

"'We are not able to go up against the people, for they are stronger than we.' And they gave the children of Israel a bad report of the land which they had spied out, saying, 'The land through which we have gone as spies is a land that devours its inhabitants, and all the people whom we saw in it are men of great stature. There we saw the giants (the descendants of Anak came from the giants); and we were like grasshoppers in our own sight, and so we were in their sight'" (Numbers 13:31-33).

Although the spies' report sounds like they saw the kinds of giants Jack met at the top of the beanstalk, the real giants in the Bible were much smaller. For instance, Og of Bashan was less than thirteen feet tall, judging by the size of his bed described in Deuteronomy 3.

Even so, to the Israelites, the giants looked invincible. And this one, Goliath, was armed to the teeth. Philistine armor was state-of-the-art. In fact, 1 Samuel 13:19-22 says the Israelites actually went to the Philistines for their metal tools and weapons. Goliath, as a champion, would have had the best armor available. His helmet and his coat of mail (or vest) were bronze. His vest alone weighed 125 pounds. The helmet weighed 20 pounds or more. His iron spearhead weighed 15 pounds, plus the shaft, which was as big as a weaver's beam. When you add his sword, javelin, and leg armor, Goliath carried at least 200 pounds of armor and weapons. No wonder the Israelites were dismayed and greatly afraid.

Notice Goliath employed a shield bearer. Shield bearers did more than just carry the shields for the soldiers. They were well-trained, disciplined combatants. They usually wore armor but carried only a small sword and a big shield. Elite soldiers and shield bearers fought as a team, with the soldier fighting on offense while the shield bearer defended him. Goliath was accustomed to fighting behind the protection of a shield bearer.

Goliath was a Philistine champion. The Hebrew word for "champion" means "one who stands between two armies." In addition, the word "Goliath" means "to capture, or place in bondage." It was a fitting name for him, considering his challenge to the Israelites, who had been freed from bondage. If he won, they would be in bondage again. If they could not find a champion of their own, they would lose by default.

However, they did not realize they already had a champion who made Goliath look like a pip squeak.

> "Do not be terrified, or afraid of them. The Lord your God, who goes before you, He will fight for you …" (Deuteronomy 1:29-30).

The Israelites heard the words of the Philistine, but they forgot the words of the Lord. Remember that the enemy giant was hemmed in between a hedge and a fence and could not cross the boundary of the blood drops. Though the giant could only shout at them, they were scared witless.

It sounds silly, doesn't it? How could they not trust the God who had consistently proven Himself to them so often in their history?

# STRATEGY: RECOGNIZE YOUR OPPONENT

What is a giant? It is anything bigger than you that stands in the way of completing the work God has given you to do, something that threatens to either make you fall or force you back into bondage. Through the eyes of the flesh, these giants seem invincible.

Here are some characteristics of typical giants:

- They appear to be bigger, better equipped, more experienced, and stronger than us.
- They seem to be unbeatable, mysterious, unnatural, and unexplainable.
- They threaten, belittle, demoralize, and terrorize us.
- They are ruthless, ungodly, loud, and irreverent.
- Yet they are awesome, magnificent, impressive, and even alluring to our flesh.

Bondage keeps us from being free to follow Christ and experience the abundant life He gives.

What spiritual giants might you face today? Corrupt governments, corporations or organizations are giants. Addictions like alcohol and drugs are giants of bondage. Remarkably, Goliath was from *Gath*, which means "winepress."

> "Harlotry, wine, and new wine enslave the heart"
> (Hosea 4:11).

Gambling leads to bondage. Pornography leads to bondage. Debt is bondage. Works-based religion (i.e., trying to be good enough to get into heaven) is bondage. Keeping up with the Joneses is bondage. Depression is bondage. Fear is bondage. You can probably think of several others to add to this list.

> "Jesus answered them, 'Most assuredly, I say to you, whoever commits sin is a slave of sin. And a slave does not abide in the house forever, but a son abides forever. Therefore, if the Son makes you free, you shall be free indeed'" (John 8:34-36).

One of my first encounters with a giant began with a message on my office answering machine—yes, that was a long time ago. It was about a week before I was to emcee the local observance of the National Day of Prayer. I was already nervous about being before the crowd. It was my first time to lead the event, which was to be held at the City Hall. Several hundred had attended the year before, and we were expecting even more this time. The mayor had prepared a proclamation, and several local leaders were scheduled to attend and lead in prayer.

The message on my machine was from a reporter at the local newspaper who wanted to interview me. Specifically, he wanted to ask me why I thought this event and the mayor's proclamation didn't violate the Constitution's separation of church and state. The tone of his voice told me that he was convinced they did. Now I really was nervous, knowing how local stories like this could become national news in the hands of an ambitious reporter. I imagined the AP headline: "Arkansas Christian Bigots Scorn the Constitution."

Before I called him back, I opened the Bible on my desk to where I had left off the day before and began reading 2 Chronicles 20. King

Jehoshaphat had received a message that a massive enemy force was about to attack his kingdom.

> "And Jehoshaphat feared and set himself to seek the Lord … and said, O Lord God of our fathers, are you not God in heaven, and do you not rule over all the kingdoms of the nations, and in Your hand is there not power and might, so that no one is able to withstand you? … O our God will You not judge them? For we have no power against this great multitude that is coming against us, nor do we know what to do, but our eyes are upon You" (2 Chronicles 20:3, 6, 12).

Those words described exactly how I felt. Even though it was only one reporter, I was convinced he was a shield bearer for the entire mainstream media. I had no idea how to handle this giant. I prayed and kept reading the verses that describe how God answered Jehoshaphat's prayer:

> "Thus says the Lord to you: Do not be afraid nor dismayed because of this great multitude, for the battle is not yours, but God's. Tomorrow go down against them … You will not need to fight in this battle. Position yourselves, stand still and see the salvation of the Lord, who is with you … Do not fear or be dismayed; tomorrow go out against them, for the Lord is with you" (2 Chronicles 20:15-17).

Convinced that God was speaking to me through His Word, I decided to wait until the next morning to return the call. That night, I prayed some more. Then I memorized the First Amendment to the Constitution.

At 8:00 AM the next day, I called the reporter. Our conversation went something like this:

"Good morning, this is Blake Watkins, and I'm returning your call. I believe you had some questions for me regarding next week's National Day of Prayer?"

"Yes, thank you. I understand that you are the person in charge of the event at the City Hall. Is this a Christian event?"

"Well, I am a Christian, but this is a national event, held annually for several years now. George Washington himself actually called for the first one while he was President, and many US presidents have since."

"How does this event not violate the constitution's requirement for the separation of church and state?"

"That's a good question. Can you tell me where, specifically, the constitution calls for that?"

"The First Amendment."

"Okay, the First Amendment says, 'Congress shall make no law respecting an establishment of religion or prohibiting the free exercise thereof; or abridging the freedom of speech, or of the press; or the right of the people peaceably to assemble, and to petition the Government for a redress of grievances.' Congress is not involved here, although there will be an event in Washington, DC, which many legislators will attend. I believe even the President will speak.

But actually, the phrase "separation of church and state" appears nowhere in the US Constitution. Although I have heard that it was in the old Soviet constitution."

"Are you going to pray?"

"I plan to, although I won't be the only one."

"Will you pray 'in Jesus' name'?"

"That's the only way I can. I have no right to approach the Creator of the universe on my own authority. But Jesus told us we could use His name."

"Will there be any non-Christians there?"

"I hope so. Everyone is welcome to come. Are you coming?"

"I don't think so."

"Can I ask you a question? … Are you a Christian? Have you ever asked Jesus to be your Lord and Savior?"

"I don't really have time to talk about that right now. Thank you for returning my call."

The article that came out the next day was very positive, although it was little more than the press release we had sent, stating the time and place for the event. We had a record crowd that year.

When you face a giant, gather strength from the Word of God.

My wife and I encountered another giant recently. His threat came in the form of a certified letter.

Jennie was involved in a wreck more than two years earlier. It nearly totaled her car, before we even made the first payment on it. She had stopped at a blind intersection. After she pulled out and almost completed her left-hand turn, her world suddenly erupted in deafening whiteness. We had no idea that SUVs have so many airbags … The mechanic later told us that seven of hers went off, each one with the sound of a twenty-gauge shotgun. She never saw the other car because all her windows were covered with limp white bags. She had been hit in the rear, driver-side door. Thankfully, nobody was seriously hurt, and the other car suffered only minor damage, though Jennie was almost deaf for several days.

After she found her purse and cell phone, which had been launched into the back floorboard, she started to call me but couldn't hear well enough to use her phone, so she handed it to a man who had stopped to help. When she asked him to call me on it, he agreed but said, "He may not answer to me." I guess he was more shaken up than she was.

Our insurance covered the damage and we didn't hear any further news about it—until we got a letter that she was being sued.

Our first instinct was fear. We imagined losing everything and going bankrupt. The legal system is bigger, better equipped, more experienced, and stronger than us. It seems unbeatable, mysterious, unnatural, and unexplainable. We felt threatened, belittled, demoralized, and terrorized. But then we recognized it was a giant.

We prayed that God would fight this battle for us—He did. When we called our insurance agency, they told us not to worry. They would resolve it. Another giant bites the dust!

〜

It is important that we recognize giants when they come against us. But how important is it that we call them by name? Many people believe that successful spiritual warfare requires us to learn and call out the names of the demons we are fighting. But what if you can't figure out what to call the giant that is threatening you?

I know of seven individual giants and at least two tribes of giants specifically mentioned in Scripture. *Anak*, *Og* of *Bashan*, *Goliath* of *Gath*, *Ishbi-Benob*, *Saph* (or *Sippai*), *Lahmi*, and the tribes of the *Zamzumim* and the *Emim*. One individual in 2 Samuel 21:20 and 1 Chronicles 20:6 is left nameless. But that didn't stop David's nephew Jonathan from defeating him. Moreover, as we will see, David always called Goliath "this Philistine." So, don't worry if you cannot name your giant.

Remarkably, the word "Goliath" can also mean "splendor." Notice how many of the giants of bondage listed above seem splendid to our fleshly nature. In fact, like the demigods of old, most people actually serve and worship them.

Someone once said that our objects of worship are whatever we:

- think about the most,
- spend the most time with,
- spend the most money on,
- are most afraid of,
- look up to the most,
- or turn to for help, protection, and provision.

"And no wonder! For Satan Himself transforms himself into an angel of light" (2 Corinthians 11:14).

Giants still fight behind shield bearers today, just as Goliath did. However, a shield bearer is not a giant. A shield bearer is a human being who aids and defends the giant. Anyone who encourages and defends sin is a shield bearer. A drug-pusher is a shield bearer for drug addiction. A pornographer is a shield bearer. Bars, liquor stores, and casinos are full of shield bearers. Anyone who wants to keep you in bondage is a shield bearer. Legalistic preachers are shield bearers. Negative people are shield bearers. Bankers, debt collectors, and government agents can be shield bearers. These people are not giants. They are human beings. They may be standing on the wrong side, but remember what Paul said,

"For we do not wrestle against flesh and blood, but against principalities, against powers, against the rulers of the darkness of this age, against spiritual hosts of wickedness in the heavenly places" (Ephesians 6:12).

Only through the Spirit can we see the truth.

"Stand fast therefore in the liberty by which Christ has made us free, and do not be entangled again with a yoke of bondage" (Galatians 5:1).

# THINK ABOUT IT—TALK ABOUT IT

**O: Recognize Your Opponent**

List some giants you have had to face or are threatening you now.

_____

How did these giants try to block you?

_____

What bondage did they threaten to force you into?

_____

Did you believe their threats? Did they succeed?

_____

What are some ways you can recognize giants?

_____

What does the name "Goliath" mean?

_____

Why is it important to know your enemy?

_____

Why is it important to understand that people are not giants?

_____

Have you ever encountered a shield bearer for a giant?

_____

# THE GOLIATH CODE

G:      Geography—Understand the Geography

O:      Opponent—Recognize Your Opponent

L:      Labels—Use the Right Labels

I:      Intrepid—Be Intrepid

A:      Aim—Aim to Please God

T:      Truth—Speak the Truth

H:      Hardware—Use the Right Hardware

C:      Confess—Confess the Lord

O:      Overcome—Overcome!

D:      Demonstrate—Demonstrate Your Faith

E:      Endure—Endure to the End

# Chapter Three

# LABELS

## HISTORY: THE HERO

"Am I not a Philistine, and you the servants of Saul?" … Now David was the son of that Ephrathite of Bethlehem Judah, whose name was Jesse, and who had eight sons. And the man was old, advanced in years, in the days of Saul. The three oldest sons of Jesse had gone to follow Saul to the battle. The names of his three sons who went to the battle were Eliab the firstborn, next to him Abinadab, and the third Shammah. David was the youngest. And the three oldest followed Saul. But David occasionally went and returned from Saul to feed his father's sheep at Bethlehem. And the Philistine drew near and presented himself forty days, morning and evening.

Then Jesse said to his son David, 'Take now for your brothers an ephah of this dried grain and these ten loaves and run to your brothers at the camp. And carry these ten cheeses to the captain of their thousand, and see how your brothers fare, and bring back news of them'" (1 Samuel 17:8b,12-18).

David was from the little town of Bethlehem, which was only twenty miles from Gath, where Goliath lived. At the time of this story, and probably unbeknownst to Saul, the prophet Samuel had already anointed young David as king. Saul's servants described David as "a mighty man of valor, a man of war, prudent in speech, and a handsome person; and the Lord is with him." (1 Samuel 16:18) He was Saul's armor bearer, according to 1 Samuel 16:21. However, he was a "weekend warrior," while his three older brothers were regular army.

Even after Samuel anointed him as king, David continued to submit to his elderly father, keeping the family sheep. And David obeyed his father when asked to deliver food to his brothers. In other words, he was serving the Lord by honoring his father.

"Children, obey your parents in all things, for this is well pleasing to the Lord" (Colossians 3:20).

The Hebrew word "David" means "loving." God is love, according to 1 John 4:16, 1 Samuel 13:14, and Acts 13:22. David is called a man after God's own heart. Judging by the way he treated his father, his king, and his Lord, his name certainly fit him at this time of his life.

No doubt he understood who he was, and he knew whom he served.

"O Lord, truly I am Your servant; I am Your servant, the son of Your maidservant; You have loosed my bonds" (Psalm 116:16).

The other Hebrews, however, did not understand or remember who they were. Goliath had called them "servants of Saul" (verse 8). They didn't disagree. Nevertheless, God had said they were His servants.

> "For the children of Israel are servants to Me; they are My servants whom I brought out of the land of Egypt: I am the LORD your God" (Leviticus 25:55).

David's brothers were probably typical of the soldiers in Saul's army. Their names remind me of three labels we could give people in churches today. *Eliab*, whose name means "the God of our fathers," was the oldest. He may have been what we call a conservative. If so, he would have preferred the old ways of doing things, strictly by the book.

*Abinadab* means "the father of liberals." The word liberal originally meant generous, but nowadays it has unfortunately taken on a political connotation.

Then there was *Shammah*. His name means "stunned" or "stupefied." He represents everyone in the middle. Moderates just try to stay between the ditches. These middle-of-the-road folks are head-on collisions waiting to happen. Tony Perkins of the Family Research Council once said, "There is nothing in the middle of the road but yellow stripes and dead animals!"

It is so tempting and natural to categorize people, such as David's brothers, using carnal labels such as these. But carnal labels only divide us.

> "Now I plead with you, brethren, by the name of our Lord Jesus Christ, that you all speak the same thing, and that

there be no divisions among you, but that you be perfectly joined together in the same mind and in the same judgment" (1 Corinthians 1:10).

# STRATEGY: USE THE RIGHT LABELS

Never let the adversary, who always lies, stick labels on you. Those labels contradict who God says you are. If we forget who we are in Christ, we will believe what the enemy says about us. We will be divided and unable to stand.

"And if a house is divided against itself, that house cannot stand" (Mark 3:25).

We will lose our focus and therefore, the battle.

~~~

The modern church is plastered with all kinds of labels: Baptist, Methodist, Church of Christ, Pentecostal, Catholic, Assemblies of God, Presbyterian, Episcopalian, Lutheran, Non-Denominational, etc. Each of these have additional labels further dividing them, such as Southern Baptist, Missionary Baptist, Landmark Baptist, Freewill Baptist, etc. Even within individual congregations, we label individuals based on politics as Democrats, Republicans, Independents, conservatives, liberals, etc.

Although these labels may seem to help us categorize and organize, I am reminded of what my evangelist-friend Jack Daniels—yes, that was his real name—said, "All those labels will either blow off on the way up or burn off on the way down!"

~~~

Are all labels bad? Not the labels God gives us.

I once heard a pastor say that Christians are righteous because God says we are. But that statement didn't sit well with me because the Bible says:

"There is none righteous, no not one" (Romans 3:10).

I had been in church all my life. I was born again at 9-years-old and later I became a licensed, Baptist minister. I was not a bad person; nevertheless, I knew I was not righteous. At best I was a "sinner saved by grace," but still a sinner.

The pastor challenged us to discover who God said we were. I had been a Christian for almost forty years at the time, yet I could only think of a handful of labels: Christian, overcomer, peculiar people, disciple, saved, sinner-saved-by-grace, etc.

His challenge caused me to ponder, study, and pray.

At the time I had just begun teaching at a successful drug and alcohol recovery ministry named John 3:16 Ministries located in Charlotte, Arkansas. It is a "spiritual boot camp" for men with addictions. For more than three years, I taught a thirteen-week, fifteen-hour-per-week course I developed on spiritual warfare, armor, and tactics (SWAT), based on Ephesians 6. During that time, we surveyed and found that two out of three men who came to the ministry "sick and tired of being sick and tired" were set free from the bondage of alcohol and drug addiction. I knew the labels that the world puts on people like the men at the ministry, labels such as failure, addict, alcoholic, drunkard, loser, and much worse.

"And such were some of you. But you were washed, but you were sanctified, but you were justified in the name of the

Lord Jesus and by the Spirit of our God" (1 Corinthians 6:11).

But these labels, while once true, no longer applied to them. As I looked in the Bible in response to the pastor's challenge, I searched the Scriptures to discover who we are now—"in Christ." I am sure I didn't find all the verses, but I was surprised and amazed when I found more than 150 descriptive labels for us in Christ!

"Sinner" was not one of them, but "righteous" is.

If you are in Christ, God does not label you a sinner anymore. He calls you a saint—though you still sin.

We need to realize the difference between what we do and who we are. You are not what you do. You are who God says you are. Period.

We've all heard the saying, "If it walks like a duck and talks like a duck, it's a duck." I don't know where that came from, but it's simply not true. It could be a baby swan ... or someone just acting like a duck.

The truth is if someone walks like a sinner and talks like a sinner, it does not necessarily mean they are a sinner. They might be a baby saint, or even an older one acting like a sinner.

In "Annex 3: Who We Are In Christ," you can read the list I compiled, with references.

Most drug and alcohol rehab ministries use the Alcoholics Anonymous twelve-step method. The original AA program was Christian and based on principles found in the Bible. However, many of these programs have become secularized to the point where Jesus Christ, the Almighty Savior of the Bible, is replaced by a "higher power" of your own choosing. Furthermore, some of these programs include the enemy's lie of "once an addict, always an addict." This lie blatantly contradicts the plain Gospel (good news) message:

> "Therefore, if anyone is in Christ, he is a new creation; old things have passed away; behold, all things have become new" (2 Corinthians 5:17).

Sadly, some Christians believe and teach the lie that certain people can never change. As such, they unwittingly agree with the devil and deny the transforming power of the Holy Spirit to remake us into new creations. Are they the ones Paul warned Timothy about?

> "Having a form of godliness but denying its power. And from such people turn away! For of this sort are those who creep into households and make captives of gullible women loaded down with sins, led away by various lusts, always learning and never able to come to the knowledge of the truth" (2 Timothy 3:5-7).

You've likely seen portrayals of a stereotypical rehab meeting, where the attendees introduce themselves with something like, "Hi, my name is so and so and I'm an alcoholic." Satan agrees with that.

The ministry of John 3:16 teaches men not to agree with the devil or say what he says. Jesus never did. He only spoke what the Father said.

> "I speak to the world those things which I heard from Him" (John 8:26).

"For I have not spoken on my own authority; but the Father who sent Me gave Me a command, what I should say and what I should speak. And I know that His command is everlasting life. Therefore, whatever I speak, just as the Father has told Me, so I speak" (John 12:49-50).

"He who does not love Me does not keep My words; and the word which you hear is not Mine but the Father's who sent Me" (John 14:24).

Since God's Word is truth, we are whatever *He* says we are.

"Sanctify them by Your truth. Your word is truth" (John 17:17).

"The entirety of Your word is truth" (Psalm 119:160).

Shortly after I compiled the list, we held the first annual Unity Fest in Batesville, Arkansas. Hundreds of supporters, family, friends and neighbors gathered on a gorgeous Saturday afternoon at Riverside Park on the White River to enjoy food, fellowship, testimonies, and Christian music. After everyone had eaten their fill of hushpuppies, fries and the best catfish ever, they gathered on lawn chairs and blankets around the large new pavilion to watch the show. Nobody anticipated what happened next.

More than two dozen residents and graduates of the ministry, plus the director and I, lined up on the outdoor gazebo stage. The boisterous crowd grew so quiet you could hear a fish flop, as one-by-one the men began to introduce themselves.

"Hi, my name is James, and I'm saved, safe, and sealed!"

"I'm Josh, and I'm a new creation!"

"Hello! I'm Tim, and I'm more than a conqueror!"

"My name is Joe, and I'm struck down, but not destroyed!"

"Hi. My name is Michael. I once was lost, but now I'm found!"

"My name is Ricky, and I'm a child of the King!"

"Hi, my name is Clay, and I'm clay in the Potter's hand."

"Hello. My name is Keith, and I'm a soldier of Jesus Christ!"

"Hi! My name is Josh, and I'm a son of the Light!"

After everyone had introduced themselves, we received a standing ovation. Napkins became handkerchiefs as tears watered the park. Rarely have I experienced more of God's presence anywhere.

For some, it was the first time they had seen their loved ones and friends since they had been set free from the bondage of sin. Many had never seen such a powerful demonstration of faith. I personally witnessed the Spirit mending torn marriages and restoring shredded families that weekend. And I have never been more thankful to see and be a part of God's work.

What a difference it makes to confess about yourself what Christ says about you.

~~~

David had been anointed by God—but so have you—if you're in Christ!

> "Now He who establishes us with you in Christ and has anointed us is God, who also has sealed us and given us the Spirit in our hearts as a guarantee" (2 Corinthians 1:21-22).

> "But you have an anointing from the Holy One" (1 John 2:20).

Never ever agree with the devil. Everything he says is a lie. He wants you to believe that you are still in bondage. Jesus said,

> "He was a murderer from the beginning, and does not stand in the truth, because there is no truth in him. When he speaks a lie, he speaks from his own resources, for he is a liar and the father of it" (John 8:44).

The power of labels is that we believe them. We tend to believe we are who we and others say we are, especially when told by people we respect or those who are supposed to love us. And it is human nature to act like who we think we are.

If you think you are an addict, failure, loser, or sinner, you will act like one.

If you understand you are a beloved child of God and His ambassador, you will act like one.

Carnal (fleshly, worldly) labels divide and discourage us. God's labels unite and encourage us.

# THINK ABOUT IT—TALK ABOUT IT

**L: Use the Right Labels**

What labels have you worn in your past?

_____

What carnal labels are you tempted to accept for yourself or others?

_____

Why is it important for us to know what labels God gives us?

_____

Why is it dangerous to use the wrong labels?

_____

Read the list "Who We Are In Christ" in the Appendix. What is your favorite God-given label? Look up the Scripture reference for it. How is it helpful for you to use this label?

_____

Why is it so hard for us to accept that we are who God says we are?

_____

How can we help others by applying the right labels to them?

_____

# THE GOLIATH CODE

G:     Geography—Understand the Geography

O:     Opponent—Recognize Your Opponent

L:     Labels—Use the Right Labels

I:     Intrepid—Be Intrepid

A:     Aim—Aim to Please God

T:     Truth—Speak the Truth

H:     Hardware—Use the Right Hardware

C:     Confess—Confess the Lord

O:     Overcome—Overcome!

D:     Demonstrate—Demonstrate Your Faith

E:     Endure—Endure to the End

# Part II

# THE WORD OF THEIR TESTIMONY

# Chapter Four

# INTREPID

## HISTORY: THE TEST

"And the Philistine drew near and presented himself forty days, morning and evening ....

Now Saul and they and all the men of Israel were in the Valley of Elah, fighting with the Philistines. So, David rose early in the morning, left the sheep with a keeper, and took the things and went as Jesse had commanded him. And he came to the camp as the army was going out to the fight and shouting for the battle. For Israel and the Philistines had drawn up in battle array, army against army. And David left his supplies in the hand of the supply keeper, ran to the army, and came and greeted his brothers.

Then as he talked with them, there was the champion, the Philistine of Gath, Goliath by name, coming up from the armies of the Philistines; and he spoke according to the same words. So, David heard them. And all the men of Israel, when they saw the man, fled from him and were dreadfully afraid. So, the men of Israel said, 'Have you seen this man who has come up? Surely, he has come up to defy Israel; and it shall be that the man who kills him the king will enrich with great riches, will give him his daughter, and give his father's house exemption from taxes in Israel.'

Then David spoke to the men who stood by him, saying, 'What shall be done for the man who kills this Philistine and takes away the reproach from Israel? For who is this uncircumcised Philistine, that he should defy the armies of the living God?' And the people answered him in this manner, saying, 'So shall it be done for the man who kills him'" (1 Samuel 17:16-27).

Have you ever noticed how often forty days is mentioned in the Bible?

- It rained forty days and nights during Noah's flood.
- Noah waited forty days after the ark came to rest on Ararat before he released the raven.
- Moses was on Mt. Sinai forty days.
- The Israelite spies were in Canaan forty days.
- Moses prostrated himself, interceding for the Israelites before the Lord for forty days.
- Elijah journeyed forty days and forty nights on the strength of angel food.
- Ezekiel lay on his side, symbolically bearing the iniquity of Judah, forty days.
- Jonah warned Ninevah forty days.

- Jesus fasted forty days and forty nights before His temptation in the wilderness.
- He walked among His followers forty days after His resurrection.
- And Goliath challenged the Israelites forty days and nights.

Forty seems to be the number that symbolizes testing, purifying, preparation, and cleansing. Here, God allowed Goliath to test Israel's faith forty days. The nation certainly needed purifying and cleansing.

God had given specific instructions to His people about what to do and how to act before a battle.

> "When you go out to battle against your enemies, and see horses and chariots and people more numerous than you, do not be afraid of them; for the LORD your God is with you, who brought you up from the land of Egypt. So it shall be, when you are on the verge of battle, that the priest shall approach and speak to the people. And he shall say to them, 'Hear, O Israel: Today you are on the verge of battle with your enemies. *Do not let your heart faint, do not be afraid, and do not tremble or be terrified* because of them; for the LORD your God is He who goes with you, to fight for you against your enemies, to save you'" (Deuteronomy 20:1-4). [Emphasis mine.]

For forty days, He tested them to see whether they had confidence in what He had said. They failed the test, miserably, and were dreadfully afraid.

Where was the priest, anyway? *Ahijah* was the high priest under Saul at the time, but there is no indication he was anywhere near the battlefield. His name means "friend of God," but he failed to do what God had commanded him. Jesus said:

"You are My friends if you do whatever I command you" (John 15:14).

Have you ever wondered why God sometimes seems to delay coming to our rescue? This passage illustrates one reason. They had no confidence in God's Word—perhaps because they didn't know it, due to the failure of their spiritual leadership—so they were trying to fight the battle their own way, in their own strength.

That never works. On our own, we are no match for any giant. Jesus warns us:

"… without Me you can do nothing" (John 15:5).

However:

"Through God we will do valiantly, for it is He who shall tread down our enemies" (Psalm 108:13).

"Be strong and of good courage, *do not fear nor be afraid* of them; for the LORD your God, He is the One who goes with you. He will not leave you nor forsake you" (Deuteronomy 31:6). [Emphasis mine.]

"Be strong and of good courage; *do not be afraid,* nor be dismayed, for the LORD your God is with you wherever you go" (Joshua 1:9). [Emphasis mine.]

David had gotten up early that morning, an absolute necessity on the day of battle. He couldn't believe his ears when he heard about the reward Saul offered. Great riches, a princess bride, and no taxes—all just for killing one little giant? Why hadn't someone jumped on this opportunity? After all, "who is this uncircumcised Philistine, that he should defy the armies of the living God?" (1 Samuel 17:26).

David recognized where he was. He understood Who his Champion was. He knew who he was. He realized that to defy God's people was to defy God Himself. And David had complete confidence that God would honor His Word.

Why didn't everyone else see this? Thinking he must have misunderstood, or heard wrong, he asked several people to verify the reward. They all said the same thing. He must have thought, "This is too good to be true." But what was wrong with the soldiers? They had stopped fighting and were now running away. Why didn't anyone else understand what David understood?

# STRATEGY: BE INTREPID; HAVE FAITH IN GOD

World War I flying ace and race-car driver Eddie Rickenbacker famously said, "Courage is doing what you are afraid of." That is difficult enough. However, God's Word repeatedly commands us "do not be afraid" and "do not fear."

More than a dozen US battleships and aircraft carriers—even a Federation starship in Star Trek—have borne the name "Intrepid." But this synonym for fearless, unafraid, undaunted, bold, daring, and brave is not often used in conversation today. I wonder if that's because it is such a rare trait in humans.

As Christians, we need to remember that no giant is a match for our Advocate.

> "You are of God, little children, and have overcome them, because He who is in you is greater than he who is in the world" (1 John 4:4).

Not only are we in Christ—He is in us!

> "For He Himself has said, 'I will never leave you nor forsake you.' So we may boldly say: 'The Lord is my helper; *I will not fear.* What can man do to me?'" (Hebrews 13:5-6). [Emphasis mine.]

As servants of the Lord Jesus (see Colossians 3:24), when the giants of bondage defy us, they actually are defying Him. But all too often when a giant hollers at us, we become dismayed and afraid, despite all Jesus' warnings.

"And *do not fear* those who kill the body but cannot kill the soul. But rather fear Him who is able to destroy both soul and body in hell" (Matthew 10:28). [Emphasis mine.]

"Are not five sparrows sold for two copper coins? And not one of them is forgotten before God. But the very hairs of your head are all numbered. *Do not fear,* therefore; you are of more value than many sparrows" (Luke 12:6-7). [Emphasis mine.]

"Watch, stand fast in the faith, be brave, be strong" (1 Corinthians 16:13).

"For God has not given us the spirit of fear, but of power, and of love, and of a sound mind" (2 Timothy 1:7).

Fear is spiritual, but it's not from God. He gives us power, love, and the ability to think.

Satan knows that the best way to dumb people down is to scare them. And giants who want to control you don't use reason. They use fear. They always use the same tactic: make you so afraid you'll gladly give up your God-given freedoms, shut up, and comply.

To be intrepid, fearless, or bold is actually the result and evidence of being filled with the Spirit.

"And when they had prayed, the place where they were assembled together was shaken; and they were all filled with the Holy Spirit, and they spoke the word of God with boldness" (Acts 4:31).

"The wicked flee when no one pursues, but the righteous are bold as a lion" (Proverbs 28:1).

How can we become truly intrepid? We begin by planting a seed of faith, of which a measure has been given to all of us in Christ (see Romans 12:3).

What is faith? Few concepts in the Bible are more misunderstood.

It is not a religious term, although these days we seem to use it exclusively as such. The word "faith" is simply a synonym for "confidence." In fact, confidence is a transliteration of the Latin words *"con,"* which means "with," and *"fide,"* which means "faith."

Try this: think of your favorite faith verses and substitute the word "confidence" for "faith."

Faith always has an object. It is always *in* something. Even atheists have faith in something, like their doctor, brakes on a car, the pilot flying their plane, chairs and step stools, or the strangers cooking their fast food and canning their vegetables.

Oftentimes this faith is not justified and we learn so when we're let down. But biblical faith is confidence in God and His Word. It is always justified because His Word is always true (see John 17:17).

I once saw a meme of a workplace, bulletin-board poster that said:

---

## NOTICE:

The beatings will continue until the morale improves.

*Management*

---

From an earthly perspective, this seems cruel and ridiculous.

Yet that is precisely what was happening here. God has given specific guidelines about how to fight His battles, and "Do not be afraid" is the first and most important. If we want the devil to stop beating us, we need God to step in and fight for us. As Moses told the Israelites on the shore of the Red Sea:

> "Do not be afraid. Stand still, and see the salvation of the Lord, which He will accomplish for you today … The Lord will fight for you, and you shall hold your peace" (Exodus 14:14).

Before He will fight for us, we must be intrepid and show confidence in Him. If our faith is weak, our faith morale must improve.

> "But without faith it is impossible to please Him, for he who comes to God must believe that He is, and that He is a rewarder of those who diligently seek Him" (Hebrews 11:6).

> "But let him ask in faith, with no doubting, for he who doubts is like a wave of the sea driven and tossed by the wind. For let not that man suppose that he will receive anything from the Lord; he is a double-minded man, unstable in all his ways" (James 1:6).

Fear and trepidation can keep you from experiencing the amazing feats God has prepared to do through you.

Why does God tell us not to fear? After all, the world is dangerous. Would it be wise for a father mouse to say to his family, "Don't be afraid of cats, snakes, mouse traps, or farmer's wives?" That would be irresponsible.

Why then is it not irresponsible for our Father God to tell us not to be afraid? Because a mouse can do nothing to protect his family from those things—unless his name is Mighty Mouse or Speedy Gonzales—so it is right for them to fear. On the other hand, our Father is Almighty God, and He has promised to help us.

> "What then shall we say to these things? If God is for us, who can be against us?" (Romans 8:31)

And faith is not blindness or ignorance. David was not ignorant of Goliath. He understood his opponent well, while knowing his God even better.

> "The Lord is my light and my salvation;
>
> Whom shall I fear?
>
> The Lord is the strength of my life;
>
> Of whom should I be afraid?
>
> When the wicked came against me to eat up my flesh,
>
> My enemies and foes, they stumbled and fell.
>
> Though an army may encamp against me,
>
> My heart shall not fear;
>
> Though war may rise against me,
>
> In this I will be confident."
>
> (Psalm 27:1-3).

Is it even possible to have no fear? Perhaps not, in these carnal bodies, but like Martin Luther said of temptation, "You cannot keep the birds from flying over your head, but you can keep them from building a nest in your hair."

What then should we do when fear flies around our heads? We swat it away. Use that initial feeling as a warning alarm. To clear it, have faith. Trust God.

"Whenever I am afraid, I will trust in You" (Psalm 56:3).

~~~

One night years ago I tossed and turned in bed, worried and afraid of what I imagined might happen the next day. We were struggling financially at the time, so I was praying while half asleep asking God why He hadn't met all our needs like He promised. After all, we were trying to follow Him and obeying Him in every way we knew how. Without turning on the light, I got up and walked down the hall to the bathroom. While still praying, I suddenly smashed my big toe into the corner of the doorpost.

Wide awake now, yet slightly delirious, I questioned God, "Why did You let me stump my toe while I was talking to You?" Before the pain subsided, I sensed His answer: "Because you are walking in the dark."

Knowing God was trying to get me to understand something important, I searched until I found this scripture:

"Who among you fears the Lord? Who obeys the voice of His servant? Who walks in darkness and has no light? Let

him trust in the name of the LORD and rely on his God"
(Isaiah 50:10).

Who fears the Lord? I do. Who obeys the voice of His Servant?
I try. Who walks in darkness and has no light? That would be me.

I realized I hadn't been praying in faith—only complaining. Not
trusting, I was worried and afraid, believing in my circumstanc-
es and questioning God, rather than trusting my all-powerful, al-
ways-faithful God and His word.

> "In God I have put my trust; I will not be afraid. What can
> man do to me?" (Psalm 56:11).

∼

Have you ever asked God for more faith? I have, at least until I realized what I was saying. If biblical faith really is confidence in God
and in His word, then what I am actually saying to God is, "Lord,
increase my confidence in You and in what You say." When I say it
like that, I realize how insulting those words must sound to Him.
What more could He do or say to give me increased confidence in
Him? How could He possibly be more trustworthy? But asking for
more faith is not the real insult. Not having faith is.

Even the apostles once asked Jesus for more faith, as recorded in the
Gospel of Luke.

> "And the apostles said to the Lord, 'Increase our faith'"
> (Luke 17:5).

I was so excited when the Spirit led me to this passage. I had prayed those same words so many times, I could hardly wait to see how Jesus answered them.

> "So the Lord said, 'If you have faith as a mustard seed, you can say to this mulberry tree, 'Be pulled up by the roots and be planted in the sea, and it would obey you'" (Luke 17:6).

Yes! That's the kind of faith I want! I want to make some trees fly (and mountains move). So, I eagerly read on to learn that kind of faith.

> "And which of you, having a servant plowing or tending sheep, will say to him when he has come in from the field, 'Come at once and sit down to eat'? But will he not rather say to him, 'Prepare something for my supper, and gird yourself and serve me till I have eaten and drunk, and afterward you will eat and drink'? Does he thank that servant because he did the things that were commanded him? I think not. So likewise you, when you have done all those things which you are commanded, say, 'We are unprofitable servants. We have done what was our duty to do'" (Luke 17:7-10).

Huh? They asked Him for more faith and He asked them questions about servants eating supper? Did I miss His answer or did He avoid the question? I read it again. Finally, it hit me. He gave an excellent answer that got right to the heart of the real issue.

The disciples thought of faith as some kind of magic they needed more of to empower them to do the cool things they wanted to do.

They first needed to humbly understand that they were servants. Only Jesus is Lord.

Once we really understand who He is, remember who we are, and understand our place in the kingdom of God, then increasing confidence in Him becomes automatic.

But we are not merely servants. Jesus also calls us His friends!

"And I say to you, *my friends, do not be afraid* ..." (Luke 12:4). [Emphasis mine.]

# THINK ABOUT IT—TALK ABOUT IT

**I: Be Intrepid**

Why is fear so dangerous?

_____

Logic says that fear can be a good thing in some situations. If that's true, why doesn't the Bible say that—or does it?

_____

How many verses can you think of that tell us to not be afraid? Which is the most meaningful to you and why?

_____

What frightens you?

_____

What should you do when you begin feeling afraid?

_____

Describe a time in your life when you were intrepid.

_____

What word is a synonym for faith?

_____

How are fear and faith related?

_____

Why is it important to have bold, Bible-teaching, spiritual leaders?

_____

# THE GOLIATH CODE

G: Geography—Understand the Geography

O: Opponent—Recognize Your Opponent

L: Labels—Use the Right Labels

I: Intrepid—Be Intrepid

A: Aim—Aim to Please God

T: Truth—Speak the Truth

H: Hardware—Use the Right Hardware

C: Confess—Confess the Lord

O: Overcome—Overcome!

D: Demonstrate—Demonstrate Your Faith

E: Endure—Endure to the End

# Chapter Five

# AIM

## HISTORY: SHIELD BUSTERS, PART 1, DISTRACTERS

"Now Eliab his oldest brother heard when he spoke to the men; and Eliab's anger was aroused against David, and he said, 'Why did you come down here? And with whom have you left those few sheep in the wilderness? I know your pride and the insolence of your heart, for you have come down to see the battle.'

And David said, 'What have I done now? Is there not a cause?' Then he turned from him toward another and said the same thing; and these people answered him as the first ones did" (1 Samuel 17:28-30).

Brothers can be your best friends or your worst rivals, especially if you are the youngest of eight, like David. The verbal exchange between big brother Eliab and his kid brother David sounds like what we might expect of sibling rivalry today. Eliab, the oldest, was a natural leader who saw this punk kid as just in his way.

Nevertheless, Eliab's anger was not justified because Jesse had told David to be there. Surely Eliab knew this, but was probably jealous of David, the baby of the family. And instead of Eliab, it was David who Samuel anointed to be the next king. To top it all off, Saul had chosen David to be his armor bearer. Eliab's jealousy made him act like a fool.

"A quick-tempered man acts foolishly" (Proverbs 14:17).

Eliab did not realize it at the time, but he was playing the part of another shield bearer for Goliath, because David had to get past him before he could get to the giant. He was David's brother and on the same side militarily, but he was acting on the enemies' behalf as an unwitting double agent. He was what Bruce Wilkinson calls a "border bully" in his best seller *The Dream Giver*. The devil was using Eliab to distract David and cause him to lose focus on his calling. Eliab was what I call a "shield buster." If he had succeeded in his ignorant sabotage, he would have destroyed David's shield of faith (see Ephesians 6:16).

Notice how David handled this distracter. Though much younger, he was wiser than Eliab. David understood these truths:

"A fool vents all his feelings, but a wise man holds them back" (Proverbs 29:11).

"A soft answer turns away wrath, but a harsh word stirs up anger" (Proverbs 15:1).

Answering wisely, you can hear the little brother in David's initial reply, "What have I done now?" But his next question spikes the ball right back into Eliab's court and refocuses the conversation.

"Isn't there a cause?" In other words, David is saying, "Isn't this cause worth fighting for?" or "Isn't this the mission God gave us?" Then David wisely turned away from the argument.

"If a wise man contends with a foolish man, whether the fool rages or laughs, there is no peace" (Proverbs 29:9).

What cause was David referring to? The Israelite mission was two-fold:

"Go in to possess the land which the Lord your God is giving you to possess" (Joshua 1:11).

"Now therefore, fear the Lord, serve Him in sincerity and in truth … Serve the Lord! … Choose you this day whom you will serve" (Joshua 24:14-15).

The Israelites were to occupy all the Promised Land and serve the Lord, not the Philistines. David understood the importance of focusing on the mission, as his son Solomon would later write,

"Let your eyes look straight ahead, and your eyelids look right before you. Ponder the path of your feet and let all your ways be established. Do not turn to the right or the left; remove your foot from evil" (Proverbs 4:25-27).

David describes his single-minded focus in Psalm 27:

"One thing I have desired of the Lord, that will I seek: That I may dwell in the house of the Lord all the days of my life, to behold the beauty of the Lord, and to inquire in His temple" (Psalm 27:4).

# STRATEGY: AIM TO PLEASE GOD

Two of the most confusing verses in the Bible are Proverbs 26:4 & 5. If not consecutive, they would be evidence to claim the Bible contradicts itself. Though Scripture never does, these two verses sure seem to:

> "Do not answer a fool according to his folly, lest you also be like him" (Proverbs 26:4).

> "Answer a fool according to his folly, lest he be wise in his own eyes" (Proverbs 26:5).

Okay, so are we supposed to answer a fool, or not? Most of the commentaries I have checked simply ignore these verses. At best, they call them a paradox, explaining sometimes we should answer a fool and other times we shouldn't. If that is the case, why did the inspired author mention this at all?

I like to read a chapter in Proverbs each day, and because there are thirty-one, I read the chapter corresponding to that day of the month. Frequently, the Holy Spirit has a providential word of wisdom for me, which is often amazing in its timing. However, on the 26th of each month, I used to struggle with these two verses. Then it hit me: We can answer a fool and not answer him at the same time if we do so with a question …

Shield busters' foolish questions are not sincere. They are not interested in learning from the answer. A shield buster's intent is to distract you so you trip and fall.

"A fool has no delight in understanding, but in expressing his own heart" (Proverbs 18:2).

If you answer foolish questions, you risk becoming a fool like him or her. But if you ignore foolish questions and refuse to answer, the fool will smugly think he or she is smarter than you.

A fool is someone who acts without thinking, despising wisdom and instruction (Proverbs 1:7) and hating knowledge (Proverbs 1:22). Success against a fool requires you causing them to think—they rarely do. Fools often drop the argument after your first thought-provoking question.

David used this tactic but Jesus perfected it. When His disciples asked honest questions, He usually answered them; yet, whenever a critic asked a question to distract or trip Him up, Jesus always answered with a question or with a statement implying a question. For instance, when they asked Him whether it was right to pay taxes to Caesar, He borrowed a coin and asked them,

> "Why do you test me? Show me a denarius (coin). Whose image and inscription does it have?" (Luke 20:23-24).

When they asked Him by whose authority He cast out demons and preached, He asked them,

> "The baptism of John—was it from heaven or from men?" (Luke 20:4).

When they asked Him whether the woman caught in adultery should be stoned, He answered,

"He who is without sin among you, let him throw a stone at her first" (John 8:7).

This was an ingenious statement, which forced each critic to ask himself the question, "Am I without sin?"

Answering with a question is an effective way to get someone to think, as when the disciples asked for more faith. Jesus also used this tactic with the rich young ruler. His question, "Good teacher, what shall I do to inherit eternal life?" was sincere, but he did not understand to whom he was talking. Therefore, Jesus answered with the question,

"Why do you call me good? No one is good but One, that is, God" (Luke 18:19).

Clearly, Jesus wanted him to think about who Jesus was—God, in the flesh.

"Walk in wisdom toward those who are outside, redeeming the time. Let your speech always be with grace, seasoned with salt, that you may know how you ought to answer each one" (Colossians 4:5-6).

I have used this tactic for years, even without fully understanding it (or Proverbs 26:4-5). As a teacher, I use the technique to get students to think for themselves. In my personal life, I use it against shield busters.

〰

One of my favorite topical-Bible studies is called "What Would Jesus Drink?" The title itself is a question. One of the main points in this message is found in Proverbs 31, which says alcohol is not for kings or princes. Since we in Christ are children of the King, I believe alcohol is not for us.

People sometimes ask me, "Why don't you drink?" Many of them, especially while I was still in school, do not really care why I abstain; they just want me to drink. I used to go into a long explanation (i.e., answering them according to their folly), but hardly ever changed anyone's mind. Now I just ask them, "Why should I?" or simply say, "I've never found a reason to." If they say, "It will help you relax," I can say, "Isn't peace a fruit of the Spirit?" If they say, "It will cheer you up," I can say, "Isn't joy a fruit of the Spirit?"

Alcohol offers us nothing except an imitation of what is already ours in Christ. If they are sincere, I can help them understand biblical reasons for abstinence. If they are not, it is best to walk away, or at least change the subject. Otherwise, I could easily lose my focus or ruin a relationship.

Be prepared for those closest to you, even your "brothers," to misunderstand you and your commitment in following the Lord. Do not be surprised if members of your family or church act as shield busters, or even shield bearers. Jesus warned us,

> "And a man's enemies will be those of his own household. He who loves father or mother more than Me is not worthy of Me. And he who loves son or daughter more than Me is not worthy of Me. And he who does not take his cross and follow after Me is not worthy of Me. He who finds his life will lose it, and he who loses his life for My sake will find it" (Matthew 10:36-39).

After more than twenty years, I left a great job as a principal engineer and supervisor at a Fortune 500 chemical company. I believed the Holy Spirit showed me it was time to choose between following my career there as an engineer and following Him. He reminded me that no one can serve two masters. And that was what I was attempting to do—serve God and the company. He has given me a passion for helping people understand that His Word is absolutely true and can be trusted. He showed me, how it has the answers for all our issues, and that He gave me the ministry of teaching. God showed me that He can change lives for the better by me teaching others what He teaches me, if only I would submit myself completely to Him and focus on Him. The more I did that, the less satisfied I became with my day job.

For a long time, I straddled the fence and prayed about what to do. But as long as I stayed where I was, I had to serve the company.

One day in June 2001, I learned that the company was going to provide an incentive package to employees who would voluntarily separate. I felt the opportunity was God's offer for me to leave that job and follow Him wherever He led. He had placed within me an irresistible desire to make an eternal difference in the lives of a lot of people. I sensed that, if I took His offer and followed Him, He would show me His power in ways I could not imagine.

> "If anyone serves Me, let him follow Me; and where I am, there My servant will be also. If anyone serves Me, him My Father will honor" (John 12:26).

In his book *Experiencing God*, Henry Blackaby said, "You cannot stay where you are and go with God."

I imagined myself on my deathbed with family around me. If I looked back on my life, which path would I wish I had chosen? I knew I would wish I had followed Jesus into the unknown. So, after twenty years, I quit my job.

Then the shield busters showed up …

"How are you going to pay your bills?" they asked. "How are you going to provide for your family?"

I replied, "Who has supplied my needs so far …the company, or God?"

They mocked, "How do you know God led you to do this? What did He sound like?"

I replied, "Have you never heard Him?"

> "Jesus said, 'My sheep hear my voice, and I know them, and they follow Me'" (John 10:27).

Jesus faced these kinds of questions too. In Matthew 12:46-48, His mother and brothers interrupted His teaching one day in an attempt to get Him to stop. He answered them with the question, "Who are my mother and brothers?"

One danger of a distraction is it causes you to forget who you really are, what your mission is, and what your vision looks like.

James says the double-minded man is unstable in all his ways.

The Bible has a lot to say about the importance of focusing.

"No one engaged in warfare entangles himself with the affairs of this life, that he may please him who enlisted him as a soldier" (2 Timothy 2:4).

If an archer allows himself to be distracted while aiming, he will miss the target. Our goal must be to aim where Jesus wants us to aim.

"Therefore we make it our *aim*, whether present or absent, to be well pleasing to Him" (2 Corinthians 5:9). [Emphasis mine.]

"*Set your mind* on things above, not on things on the earth" (Colossians 3:2). [Emphasis mine.]

"Therefore, whether you eat or drink, or whatever you do, do all to the glory of God" (1 Corinthians 10:31).

"Brethren, I do not count myself to have apprehended; but one thing I do, forgetting those things which are behind and *reaching forward* to those things which are ahead, I press toward the goal for the prize of the upward call of God in Christ Jesus" (Philippians 2:13-14). [Emphasis mine.]

"Therefore we also, since we are surrounded by so great a cloud of witnesses, let us lay aside every weight, and the sin which so easily ensnares us, and let us run with endurance the race that is set before us, *looking unto Jesus*, the author and finisher of our faith" (Hebrews 12:1-2). [Emphasis mine.]

What happens in a foot race if a runner turns to look at the other runners or the crowd? He will lose the prize and might trip or fall. I'm not a runner. Winning a race was never an issue for me, since I was usually bringing up the rear. And the guys in front of me would sometimes turn around to see who was making that weird, flapping sound—my flat feet were no fun in junior high.

In his book *Seven Habits of Highly Effective People*, with at least two of his seven habits, author Stephen Covey stresses the importance of aiming at or focusing on the mission. He says, "Begin with the end in mind" and "First things first." As Christians, the end we should have in mind is to hear our Lord say,

> "Well done, good and faithful servant … Enter into the joy of your Lord" (Matthew 25:21).

What are our first things?

> "But seek first the kingdom of God, and His righteousness, and all these things shall be added unto you" (Matthew 6:33).

# THINK ABOUT IT—TALK ABOUT IT

### A: Aim to Please God

What is a shield buster, and why are they called that?

_____

Have you ever known a distracting shield buster?

_____

What are some distractions that affect you?

_____

How can you answer a fool without answering them?

_____

Which verses regarding focusing are the most meaningful to you?

_____

Why is answering with a question so effective when dealing with shield busters?

_____

What is your "cause?"

_____

# THE GOLIATH CODE

G:      Geography—Understand the Geography

O:      Opponent—Recognize Your Opponent

L:      Labels—Use the Right Labels

I:      Intrepid—Be Intrepid

A:      Aim—Aim to Please God

T:      Truth—Speak the Truth

H:      Hardware—Use the Right Hardware

C:      Confess—Confess the Lord

O:      Overcome—Overcome!

D:      Demonstrate—Demonstrate Your Faith

E:      Endure—Endure to the End

# Chapter Six

# TRUTH

## HISTORY: SHIELD BUSTERS, PART 2, DECEIVERS

"Now when the words which David spoke were heard, they reported them to Saul; and he sent for him. Then David said to Saul, 'Let no man's heart fail because of him; your servant will go and fight with this Philistine.' And Saul said to David, 'You are not able to go against this Philistine to fight with him; for you are a youth, and he a man of war from his youth.'

But David said to Saul, 'Your servant used to keep his father's sheep, and when a lion or a bear came and took a lamb out of the flock, I went out after it and struck it, and delivered the lamb from its mouth; and when it arose against me, I caught it by its beard, and struck and killed it. Your servant has killed both lion and bear; and this uncircumcised Philistine will be like one of them, seeing he has defied the armies of the living God.' Moreover David said, 'The Lord, who delivered me from the paw of the lion and from the paw of the bear, He will deliver me from the hand of this Philistine.' And Saul said to David, 'Go, and the Lord be with you!'" (1 Samuel 17:31-37).

God had warned the people what it would be like to have a king.

"So Samuel told all the words of the Lord to the people who asked him for a king. And he said, 'This will be the behavior of the king who will reign over you: He will take your sons and appoint them for his own chariots and to be his horsemen, and some will run before his chariots. He will appoint captains over his thousands and captains over his fifties, will set some to plow his ground and reap his harvest, and some to make his weapons of war and equipment for his chariots. He will take your daughters to be perfumers, cooks, and bakers. And he will take the best of your fields, your vineyards, and your olive groves, and give them to his servants. He will take a tenth of your grain and your vintage, and give it to his officers and servants. And he will take your male servants, your female servants, your finest young men, and your donkeys, and put them to his work. He will take a tenth of your sheep. And you will be his servants. And you will cry out in that day because of your king whom you have chosen for yourselves, and the Lord will not hear you in that day.'

Nevertheless the people refused to obey the voice of Samuel; and they said, 'No, but we will have a king over us, that we also may be like all the nations, and that our king may judge us and go out before us and fight our battles'" (1 Samuel 8:10-20).

The Lord had led Samuel to anoint a young man named Saul (which, how fittingly, means "demanding").

"There was not a more handsome person than he [Saul] among the children of Israel. From his shoulders upward he was taller than any of the people" (1 Samuel 9:2).

You could say he was a "giant" among the Israelites. However, as it turned out, he was the second shield buster David had to face before he could fight Goliath.

Prior to fighting the giant everyone was afraid of, he first had to get past the "giant" everyone respected—the demanding giant of doubt.

As with all shield busters, Saul seemed to be on God's side, but he did not speak with the voice of truth. In fact, if the devil himself could have talked to David, he would have said the same thing Saul said, "You are not able to go against this Philistine to fight with him."

Saul was right, of course, if you only consider the flesh. By himself, David was not able to go against the giant. He would be squashed like a bug. But Saul had forgotten what the Spirit can do. Therefore, what he said was not true, which makes it a lie—even if he didn't know or intend it to be.

David responded by reciting his past victories over a lion and a bear, which at first sounded prideful and almost arrogant.

However, David gave God full credit for delivering him from the wild animals. This is not pride. It is confidence—faith.

# STRATEGY: SPEAK THE TRUTH

Sometimes the toughest shield busters are the so-called authorities or experts everyone respects. They are not fools, and usually don't even dignify you with a question. They just come right out with a statement of "fact" designed by Satan to put you down or stop you in your tracks. Unlike the first shield busters (the distracters), these shield busters are deceivers.

The Bible calls them scoffers or mockers. What they say often directly contradicts the plain teaching of the Word of God. For instance, when they say, "You are not able to fight this giant," they are denying the truth.

> "I can do all things through Christ who strengthens me" (Philippians 4:13).

The danger of deception is that it causes you to doubt or distort who you are, what your mission is, and what your vision looks like.

Satan also uses shield busters to tempt us to sin. One of my students at John 3:16 Ministries had been my friend in grade school, before he dropped out. After a lifetime of alcohol and drug abuse, he checked into the ministry and became radically saved. Like so many other men there, Terry became an eager student of the Word and a powerful witness for Christ's power to set us free from the bondage of sin. In his testimony he said that, for most of his life, he didn't want to live, but was afraid to die. Then since accepting Jesus as Lord, he wanted to live—and was *not* afraid to die.

After he graduated from the ministry, Terry was hungry for fellowship, and wanted to hang out with Christian men as much as possible. Knowing his story, one evening men from his church invited him to go out to eat with them. They ended up taking him to a local private club and promptly started drinking.

Even though he objected, they convinced him it was not wrong for him to drink since he had been set free from alcoholism and drug addiction and was now under grace. So, he got drunk.

Even before he sobered up, Satan attacked: "See, you're not really changed. You're still an alcoholic who can't live without drinking. God will never forgive you now. You're a hypocrite, no child of the King, and not even saved." That began a devastating downward spiral for him.

Although they may not have realized it, in this instance, these church members acted as shield busters for the enemy, and they caused Terry to fall.

What they told him was only partly true. As the Apostle Paul said,

> "All things are lawful for me, but not all things are helpful; all things are lawful for me, but not all things edify" (1 Corinthians 10:23).

The truth in Christ and under grace is that all things are legal, but not all are good for me. Some are stupid.

> "Wine is a mocker, strong drink a brawler, and whoever is intoxicated by it is not wise" (Proverbs 20:1, NASB).

The Director of John 3:16 Ministries explained it something like this, "If a born-again new creation in Christ gets drunk, it's not because he's still an alcoholic. It's because he's being stupid."

According to John 1:14, Jesus was "full of grace and truth."

> "For the law was given through Moses, but grace and truth came through Jesus Christ" (John 1:17).

Grace without truth is license. Truth without grace is legalism.

But the combination of grace and truth is love.

I heard about what happened to Terry from other church members who knew him. "Have you heard about Terry? He fell off the wagon …" "I guess John 3:16 didn't work for him …" This totally discouraged me until I realized they were shield busters. So, I asked them whether they were praying for him and reminded them of this promise:

> "Being confident of this very thing, that He who began a good work in you will be faithful to complete it until the day of Jesus Christ" (Philippians 1:6).

I knew first-hand that the good work God had begun in Terry was real. Thankfully, Terry recognized his plight and Satan's lies, remembered who he was and how to get back up. He turned back to the Lord for help.

> "For a righteous man may fall seven times and rise up …" (Proverbs 24:16).

> "Therefore let us not judge one another anymore, but rather resolve this, not to put a stumbling block or a cause to fall in our brother's way" (Romans 14:13).

〜

Perhaps the best way to handle a deceiving shield buster is to say what God has said in His Word and what He has done for you in the past. In other words, speak the Truth, and tell your testimony.

> "If you abide in My word, you are My disciples indeed. And you shall know the truth, and the truth shall make you free" (John 8:31-32).

> "Your word I have hidden in my heart, that I might not sin against You" (Psalm 119:11).

~~~

The late Dr. Adrian Rogers once said, "A Christian with a testimony is never at the mercy of an unbeliever with an argument."

> "I will remember the works of the Lord; Surely I will remember Your wonders of old. I will also meditate on all Your work, and talk of Your deeds" (Psalm 77:11-12).

> "Oh, give thanks to the Lord! Call upon His name; Make known His deeds among the peoples! Sing to Him, sing psalms to Him; Talk of all His wondrous works! Glory in His holy name; Let the hearts of those rejoice who seek the Lord! Seek the Lord and His strength; Seek His face evermore! Remember His marvelous works which He has done, His wonders, and the judgments of His mouth, O seed of Abraham His servant, You children of Jacob, His chosen ones!" (Psalm 105:1-6).

# THINK ABOUT IT—TALK ABOUT IT

**T: Speak the Truth**

Have you ever had to confront a deceiver?

_____

Are shield busters our enemies?

_____

What are some deceptions that have affected you?

_____

What is truth?

_____

Why is your testimony so powerful when dealing with shield busters?

_____

List some things God has done for you.

_____


Grace without truth is _____.

Truth without grace is _____.

Truth with grace is _____.

# THE GOLIATH CODE

G:    Geography—Understand the Geography

O:    Opponent—Recognize Your Opponent

L:    Labels—Use the Right Labels

I:    Intrepid—Be Intrepid

A:    Aim—Aim to Please God

T:    Truth—Speak the Truth

H:    Hardware—Use the Right Hardware

C:    Confess—Confess the Lord

O:    Overcome—Overcome!

D:    Demonstrate—Demonstrate Your Faith

E:    Endure—Endure to the End

# Chapter Seven

# HARDWARE

## HISTORY: THE WEAPONS

"So Saul clothed David with his armor, and he put a bronze helmet on his head; he also clothed him with a coat of mail. David fastened his sword to his armor and tried to walk, for he had not tested them. And David said to Saul, 'I cannot walk with these, for I have not tested them.' So David took them off. Then he took his staff in his hand; and he chose for himself five smooth stones from the brook, and put them in a shepherd's bag, in a pouch which he had, and his sling was in his hand. And he drew near to the Philistine" (1 Samuel 17:38-40).

In verse 37, King Saul had actually sounded godly. At least He finally said the right thing: "Go, and the Lord be with you." Then he slipped back into the flesh and gave David his armor. That seems like a logical, natural, even gracious thing to do, since David apparently had no armor of his own, at least not with him. Nevertheless, it illustrates the spiritual cluelessness of Saul at this point in his life.

Saul didn't recognize that this was a spiritual battle. His armor was carnal, just like its owner, and would be worse than useless to David in spiritual warfare. But David dutifully accepted and put on the armor Saul offered.

Undoubtedly, this was the best armor available in Israel, since it belonged to the king. But it just would not do. Your mental picture of this classic scene is likely one of a small boy with a coat of mail hanging below his knees, his sword dragging the ground, and little David peeking out from under the helmet that was swallowing his head.

However, that is not the picture Scripture portrays. Remember, one of Saul's servants had earlier described David as:

> "… a mighty man of valor, a man of war, prudent in speech, and a handsome person; and the Lord is with him" (1 Samuel 16:18).

And he had already killed at least one lion and bear. That does not describe a small boy.

Scripture is also clear that Saul's armor would not work for David because he had not tested it. In other words, he had not trained in it, fought in it, or even once used it. The heavy armor would have hindered him in the battle, so he took it off.

Then he picked up his staff, which he *had* tested on both a lion and a bear. His sling was already in his hand, ready for use. These were the weapons he had used in the battles he recounted in verse 35.

His tactic had always been to strike the enemy with a stone from his sling, grab it by the beard, and finish it with the hardened business end of his staff.

As he crossed the brook which separated the Philistines from the Israelites, he stooped and carefully selected five smooth stones to use as ammunition for his sling.

Why five? In case he missed four times? Did he think it might take more than one to kill the giant? No. According to 2 Samuel 21 and 1 Chronicles 20, Goliath had four brothers. I think they were there that day and David may have seen them in the background, dwarfing the other Philistine soldiers. He probably assumed they would rush to their brother's aid after David defeated Goliath, so he might also have to take them out. Five giants—five stones. No problem. That's confidence.

# STRATEGY: USE THE RIGHT HARDWARE

"For though we walk in the flesh, we do not war according to the flesh. For the weapons of our warfare are not carnal but mighty in God for pulling down strongholds, casting down arguments and every high thing that exalts itself against the knowledge of God, bringing every thought into captivity to the obedience of Christ" (2 Corinthians 10:3-5).

How often do we talk the Christian talk, saying all the right things—even from the pulpits and podiums of our churches—but when it is time to fight, we choose carnal weapons for spiritual battles?

As Christians, all our battles are spiritual. Even though we "walk in the flesh, we do not war according to the flesh." Carnal armor is less than useless for us in spiritual battles. It may actually hinder our success.

"Finally, my brethren, be strong in the Lord and in the power of His might. Put on the whole armor of God, that you may be able to stand against the wiles of the devil. For we do not wrestle against flesh and blood, but against principalities, against powers, against the rulers of the darkness of this age, against spiritual hosts of wickedness in the heavenly places.

Therefore take up the whole armor of God, that you may be able to withstand in the evil day, and having done all, to stand" (Ephesians 6:10-13).

Why would we ever want to use inferior weapons (even if they are the best the world has to offer), instead of the mighty spiritual weapons God has provided us?

Let's consider the armor and weapons we have available.

"Stand therefore, having girded your waist with truth, having put on the breastplate of righteousness, and having shod your feet with the preparation of the gospel of peace; above all, taking the shield of faith with which you will be able to quench all the fiery darts of the wicked one. And take the helmet of salvation, and the sword of the spirit, which is the word of God; praying always with all prayer and supplication in the Spirit, being watchful to this end with all perseverance and supplication for all the saints" (Ephesians 6:14-18).

There are seven pieces of armor listed in Ephesians 6. Seven is the number of perfection or completion. Listed in order, they are:

## The Belt of Truth

"Therefore, putting away lying, let each one of you speak truth with his neighbor, for we are members of one another" (Ephesians 4:25).

"Do not lie to one another, since you have put off the old man with his deeds, and have put on the new man who is renewed in knowledge according to the image of Him who created him" (Colossians 3:9).

If you are in Christ, the truth is you are not who you used to be (the "old man"). You are a new creation (the "new man") with new spiritual knowledge, recreated in the image of God. Speak that.

## The Breastplate of Righteousness

I call this piece of hardware the "Breastplate of Right-Choice-ness." Our choices between right and wrong do matter, even under grace, according to the New Testament.

Here are some of the wrong things that the Apostle Paul says we should no longer choose:

> "Therefore put to death your members which are on the earth: fornication, uncleanness, passion, evil desire, and covetousness, which is idolatry. Because of these things the wrath of God is coming upon the sons of disobedience, in which you yourselves once walked when you lived in them. But now you yourselves are to put off all these: anger, wrath, malice, blasphemy, filthy language out of your mouth" (Colossians 3:5-8).

Here are some right choices we should make:

> "Therefore as the elect of God, holy and beloved, put on tender mercies, kindness, humility, meekness, longsuffering" (Colossians 3:12).

## The Shoes of the Gospel of Peace

> "If it is possible, as much as depends on you, live peaceably with all men" (Romans 12:18).

"And let the peace of God rule in your hearts, to which you were called in one body; and be thankful" (Colossians 3:15).

Shoes of peace seems like a strange name for battle armor. However, the gospel of peace is not the absence of conflict. It is the presence of God.

## The Shield of Faith

As we discussed earlier, faith is confidence that God is who He says He is, that He does what He says He will do, and that what He says will happen will surely happen. Faith is confidence in God's Word.

"But without faith it is impossible to please Him, for he who comes to God must believe that He is, and that He is a rewarder of those who diligently seek Him" (Hebrews 11:6).

I believe that we best vocalize our faith by calling out Jesus' name and by telling Him, "Thank you."

"And whatever you do in word or deed, do all in the name of the Lord Jesus, giving thanks to God the Father through Him" (Colossians 3:17).

"Giving thanks always for all things to God the Father in the name of our Lord Jesus Christ" (Ephesians 5:20).

Thankfulness in the middle of the battle is a powerful expression of faith.

## The Helmet of Salvation

The helmet protects our minds and keeps our eyes focused ahead.

"Set your mind on things above, not on things on the earth" (Colossians 3:2).

"And be renewed in the spirit of your mind" (Ephesians 4:23).

"And do not be conformed to this world, but be transformed by the renewing of your mind, that you may prove what is that good and acceptable and perfect will of God" (Romans 12:2).

## The Sword of the Spirit, which is the Word of God

This weapon is a bit confusing at first. The Holy Spirit is not a sword. The Word of God is the sword.

> "For the word of God is living and powerful, and sharper than any two-edged sword, piercing even to the division of soul and spirit, and of joints and marrow, and is a discerner of the thoughts and intents of the heart" (Hebrews 4:12).

Plus, it is not my sword. It belongs to the Holy Spirit. If the Bible were my sword, I would misuse it and attack the wrong things at the wrong time and in the wrong way. As a lightsaber wielded by a Jedi knight is most effective when controlled by the Force, so too is the Word of God most effective when the Spirit guides its use. The Apostle Paul set the example:

> "And my speech and my preaching were not with persuasive words of human wisdom, but in demonstration of the Spirit and of power, that your faith should not be in the wisdom of men but in the power of God" (1 Corinthians 2:4-5).

And like a lightsaber, it shines in the dark!

"Your word is a lamp to my feet and a light to my path" (Psalm 119:105).

## The Walkie-Talkie of Prayer

The seventh piece of armor is often not included in lists or commentaries of Ephesians 6, perhaps because Paul didn't illustrate it with anything a first-century soldier would wear or carry. Yet it is just as essential and powerful as the other six.

We use the walkie-talkie of prayer to stay in contact with our King.

"Continue earnestly in prayer, being vigilant in it with thanksgiving" (Colossians 4:2).

We use it to communicate our needs and concerns.

"Be anxious for nothing, but in everything by prayer and supplication, with thanksgiving, let your requests be made known to God" (Philippians 4:6).

"So I say to you, ask, and it will be given to you; seek, and you will find; knock, and it will be opened to you" (Luke 11:9).

We use it to receive our instructions for the battle.

"Your ears will hear a word behind you saying, "This is the way, walk in it," whenever you turn to the right hand or whenever you turn to the left" (Isaiah 30:21).

"Call to Me and I will answer you and show you great and mighty things which you know not" (Jeremiah 33:3).

And like forward observers, we use it to call down holy artillery fire on the spiritual forces of darkness.

> "Call upon Me in the day of trouble; I will deliver you, and you shall glorify Me" (Psalm 50:15).

> "The effective, fervent prayer of a righteous man avails much" (James 5:16b).

Prayer *is* the battle.

I call it a walkie-talkie instead of a cell phone because we cannot talk and listen at the same time. To hear God's still, small voice you have to take your thumb off the push-to-talk button.

~~~

But doesn't the fact that we are in Jesus negate the need for armor? If we are in the impenetrable-shelter of Christ, why does Paul tell us to also put on the armor of God? Actually, there is no contradiction here at all: the spiritual armor described in Ephesians 6 is Christ Himself.

The moment you received Jesus as your Lord and Savior, the Holy Spirit placed you in Christ. The Apostle Paul also calls this "putting on Christ":

> "For as many of you as were baptized into Christ have put on Christ" (Galatians 3:27).

"Baptized" simply means "placed into." In both Romans and Ephesians, He makes it clear that putting on the armor is synonymous with putting on Christ.

"The night is far spent, the day is at hand. Therefore let us cast off the works of darkness, and put on the armor of light … But put on the Lord Jesus, and make no provision for the flesh, to fulfill its lusts" (Romans 13:12 & 14)

"Finally, my brethren, be strong in the Lord and in the power of His might. Put on the whole armor of God …" (Ephesians 6:10-11).

Amazingly, each piece of armor corresponds to one of the names of Christ. For instance:

## The Belt of Truth

Jesus is Truth.

"Jesus said to him, 'I am the way, the truth, and the life. No one comes to the Father except through Me" (John 14:6).

Truth is a person.

## The Breastplate of Righteousness

Christ is our righteousness.

"In His days Judah will be saved, and Israel will dwell safely; Now this is His name by which He will be called: The Lord Our Righteousness" (Jeremiah 23:6).

"But of Him you are in Christ Jesus, who became for us wisdom from God and righteousness and sanctification and redemption" (1 Corinthians 1:30).

## The Shoes of the Gospel of Peace

In addition to being the Prince of Peace (Isaiah 9:6), He is our peace.

"For He Himself is our peace, who has made both one, and has broken down the middle wall of separation …" (Ephesians 2:14).

"Peace I leave with you, My peace I give to you; not as the world gives do I give to you. Let not your heart be troubled, neither let it be afraid" (John 14:27).

"And the God of peace will crush Satan under your feet shortly. The grace of our Lord Jesus Christ be with you. Amen" (Romans 16:20).

## The Shield of Faith

Christ is our shield and our confidence.

"You are my hiding place and my shield; I hope in your word" (Psalm 119:114).

"The Lord is my rock and my fortress and my deliverer; My God, my strength, in whom I will trust; my shield and the horn of my salvation, my stronghold" (Psalm 18:2).

"By awesome deeds in righteousness You will answer us, O God of our salvation, You who are the confidence of all the ends of the earth" (Psalm 65:5).

## The Helmet of Salvation

Jesus' name in Hebrew is *Yeshu'a*, which means "The Lord is Salvation."

So, the Helmet of Salvation is literally the Helmet of *Yeshu'a*.

Christ the Lord is our salvation.

> "Behold, God is my salvation, I will trust and not be afraid; For *YAH*, the Lord is my strength and song; He also has become my salvation" (Isaiah 12:2).

> "The Lord is my light and my salvation; Whom shall I fear? The Lord is the strength of my life, of whom shall I be afraid?" (Psalm 27:1)

## The Sword of the Spirit (The Word of God)

The Apostle John calls Jesus "the Word."

> "In the beginning was the Word, and the Word was with God, and the Word was God" (John 1:1).

> "And the Word became flesh and dwelt among us, and we beheld His glory, the glory of the only begotten of the Father, full of grace and truth" (John 1:14).

> "He was clothed with a robe dipped in blood, and His name is called The Word of God" (Revelation 19:13).

## The Walkie-Talkie of Prayer

A walkie-talkie is simply a means of communication, serving as an electronic translator between spoken words and radio signals. Jesus Himself is our means of communication with the Father. He serves as our Spiritual Mediator between God and man. We have access to the Father only in His name.

> "For through Him we both have access by one Spirit to the Father" (Ephesians 2:18).

> "It is Christ who died, and furthermore is also risen, who is even at the right hand of God, who also makes intercession for us" (Romans 8:34).

> "Most assuredly, I say to you, whatever you ask the Father in My name He will give you" (John 16:23).

Jesus *is* the Armor of God.

~~~

The emphasis in Ephesians 6 is on the *whole* armor. All too often we Christians try to get by with only part of it. For instance, we like the helmet of salvation because we don't want to go hell. But we may ignore or neglect truth, righteousness, faith, peace, prayer and the Word of God.

Even spiritual hardware is of little benefit to us if we have not tested it. This is why we need to envision putting on all of the armor (Him) every day. Otherwise, we end up fighting in our "spiritual underwear." We must use our spiritual weapons to fight all our battles, so we get comfortable with it. Our everyday smaller battles are training opportunities for the less-frequent, major, giant fights.

When the giants do come along, we can fight them in the same way, using the same armor and weapons we used to fight the daily lions and bears.

# THINK ABOUT IT—TALK ABOUT IT

### H: Use the Right Hardware

Why couldn't David use Saul's armor?

_____

What is the belt of truth?

_____

How is the breastplate of righteousness like "right-choice-ness?"

_____

Peace is not the _____ of conflict. It is the _____ of God.

_____

How is being thankful an expression of faith?

_____

What does the helmet protect?

_____

Why is the Word called the sword of the Spirit?

_____

How is the walkie-talkie of prayer different from a cell phone?

_____

How does it help to realize that Jesus is the Armor of God?

_____

# THE GOLIATH CODE

G:     Geography—Understand the Geography

O:     Opponent—Recognize Your Opponent

L:     Labels—Use the Right Labels

I:     Intrepid—Be Intrepid

A:     Aim—Aim to Please God

T:     Truth—Speak the Truth

H:     Hardware—Use the Right Hardware

C:     Confess—Confess the Lord

O:     Overcome—Overcome!

D:     Demonstrate—Demonstrate Your Faith

E:     Endure—Endure to the End

# Chapter Eight

# CONFESS

## HISTORY: OPENING SALVO

"So the Philistine came, and began drawing near to David, and the man who bore the shield went before him. And when the Philistine looked about and saw David, he disdained him; for he was only a youth, ruddy and good-looking. So the Philistine said to David, 'Am I a dog, that you come to me with sticks?' And the Philistine cursed David by his gods. And the Philistine said to David, 'Come to me, and I will give your flesh to the birds of the air and the beasts of the field!'

"Then David said to the Philistine, 'You come to me with a sword, with a spear, and with a javelin. But I come to you in the name of the LORD of hosts, the God of the armies of Israel, whom you have defied.

'This day the LORD will deliver you into my hand, and I will strike you and take your head from you. And this day I will give the carcasses of the camp of the Philistines to the birds of the air and the wild beasts of the earth, that all the earth may know that there is a God in Israel. Then all this assembly shall know that the LORD does not save with sword and spear; for the battle is the LORD's, and He will give you into our hands'" (1 Samuel 17:41-47).

In verse 40, the Bible said David drew near to the Philistine. Now we see the Philistine drawing near to David. If this had been a movie, you would hear and feel the tension building in the soundtrack, as they each move closer and closer together. Neither is afraid, although one of them is about to die. Both had "faith." Each is confident.

Notice this passage again specifically mentions Goliath's shield bearer.

When Goliath got close enough to see David more clearly, he grew even more self-confident. This Israelite champion was no battle-scarred, hardened warrior. He was just a young man, apparently armed with only a staff. Incredulous, he shouted out to David, "Am I a dog, that you come to me with sticks?" He could not see the invisible—yet invincible—spiritual armor David wore. Nor did he sense the true power in the One who was coming against him. So, he cursed David by his gods.

A pagan curse ordinarily would strike fear into the heart of whoever happened to be on the receiving end of it. The occult is not to be trifled with and their curses were not to be taken lightly. The gods of the Philistines were really demons that had actual, but limited, supernatural power.

"Rather, that the things which the Gentiles sacrifice they sacrifice to demons and not to God, and I do not want you to have fellowship with demons" (1 Corinthians 10:20).

Even today, superstitious people are concerned about curses and spells—but not David.

He must have understood God's promise to him as a true child of Abraham.

"I will bless those who bless you, And I will curse him who curses you; And in you all the families of the earth shall be blessed" (Genesis 12:3).

He understood one indication of a wicked, ungodly person:

"His mouth is full of cursing and deceit and oppression; under his tongue is trouble and iniquity" (Psalm 10:7).

The Apostle Paul would later paraphrase this in a famous Romans 3 passage that describes the unrighteous:

"Whose mouth is full of cursing and bitterness" (Romans 3:14).

David knew God would curse Goliath, believing that the ungodly will fail.

"The ungodly are not so, but are like the chaff which the wind drives away, Therefore the ungodly shall not stand in the judgment, nor sinners in the congregation of the righteous. For the Lord knows the way of the righteous, but the way of the ungodly will perish" (Psalm 1:4-6).

David's son Solomon would later write,

> "If the righteous will be recompensed on the earth, how much more the ungodly and the sinner" (Proverbs 11:31).

> "Like a fluttering bird or like a flying swallow, so a curse without cause does not come to rest" (Proverbs 26:2).

So, David responded by boldly proclaiming to the Philistine,

> "You come to me with a sword, with a spear, and with a javelin. But I come to you in the name of the LORD of hosts, the God of the armies of Israel, whom you have defied" (1 Samuel 17:45).

Goliath had invoked his demonic gods to curse David, but David spoke the name of the Lord, the God of the armies of Heaven, who later said in Isaiah 54:15-17,

> "Indeed they shall surely assemble, but not because of Me. Whoever assembles against you shall fall for your sake. 'Behold, I have created the blacksmith who blows the coals in the fire, who brings forth an instrument for his work; and I have created the spoiler to destroy. No weapon formed against you shall prosper, and every tongue which rises against you in judgment you shall condemn. This is the heritage of the servants of the Lord, and their righteousness is from Me,' says the Lord."

The Philistines may have been famous for their metalworking skills and weapons, but David served the God who made the blacksmiths themselves. David knew he had nothing to fear; in fact, earlier he had told Saul that the Lord would deliver him from the hand of the Philistine. Now he declares the Lord will deliver the Philistine to him.

# STRATEGY: CONFESS THE LORD

As servants of the Lord Jesus, we should never forget Satan's weapons are no match for the weapons God provides. He will come at us, but we have the invincible armor of God. In addition, we have a weapon that strikes fear into the wicked heart of every demon—the name above every name, Jesus.

> "Some trust in chariots, and some in horses; but we will remember the name of the LORD our God" (Psalm 20:7).

> "The name of the LORD is a strong tower; the righteous run to it and are safe" (Proverbs 18:10).

No weapon formed against us will prosper. That is our heritage as servants of the Lord. Nevertheless, we must confess it. There is power in our words. What we say matters.

> "Life and death are in the power of the tongue" (Proverbs 18:21).

> "But I say to you that for every idle word men may speak, they will give account of it on the day of judgment. For by your words you will be justified, and by your words you will be condemned" (Matthew 12:36-37).

> "If you confess with your mouth the Lord Jesus, and believe in your heart that God has raised Him from the dead, you will be saved. For with the heart one believes unto righteousness, and with the mouth confession is made unto salvation" (Romans 10:9-10).

"For whoever calls on the name of the LORD shall be saved'" (Romans 10:13).

I can imagine God calling all the angels of heaven together and telling them, "Watch this. See my servant David down there? This is going to be good." He will say the same thing about you—if you confess Him in the battle.

> "Also I say to you, whoever confesses Me before men, him the Son of Man also will confess before the angels of God. But he who denies Me before men will be denied before the angels of God" (Luke 12:8).

> "Let the redeemed of the LORD say so, whom He has redeemed from the hand of the enemy" (Psalm 107:2).

When David was close enough to be heard, notice that he spoke directly to the giant and ignored the shield bearer. Likewise, we should boldly and directly speak to our spiritual giants of bondage, rather than wasting time on their human defenders. We must recognize our authority, which is what Jesus said in the gospels.

> "Assuredly, I say to you, if you have faith and do not doubt, you will not only do what was done to the fig tree, but also if you say to this mountain, 'Be removed and be cast into the sea', it will be done" (Matthew 21:21).

> "Behold I give you the authority to trample on serpents and scorpions, and over all the power of the enemy, and nothing shall by any means hurt you" (Luke 10:19) [Emphasis mine.]

When they come against us, we can proclaim that they actually are defying the Lord of Hosts, and we have all the armies of heaven at our backs.

> "He who hears you hears Me, he who rejects you rejects Me, and he who rejects Me rejects Him who sent Me" (Luke 10:16).

~~~

My paternal grandfather was a Baptist preacher who served as a church planter and interim pastor in North Arkansas. I had the privilege of spending the last two weeks of his life with him. He was under hospice care during the day, but my wife and I stayed with him at night. He was in a lot of pain and slept fitfully. I couldn't comprehend why God would allow one of His servants to suffer in that way. I prayed that God would comfort Grandpa. Then God spoke to me—not audibly, but clearly, as if to say, "Comforting him is your job" (see 2 Corinthians 1:4).

Later, in the middle of the night, Grandpa sat straight up in bed and yelled with wide-eyed panic at something near the ceiling in the corner of the room. My wife and I jumped up and my aunt came running.

Remembering God's admonition, I turned to where he was looking and said, "In the name of Jesus Christ, leave this man alone. He belongs to Jesus, this home is dedicated to God, and you have no right to be here." Almost immediately, Grandpa relaxed and went to sleep. He slept peacefully from then on.

"Call upon Me in the day of trouble; I will deliver you, and you shall glorify Me" (Psalm 50:15).

～

Not only can we claim deliverance from our giants, but He will also deliver our giants to us!

"Yet in all these things we are more than conquerors through Him who loved us" (Romans 8:37).

Why? Because our Father loves us. If any bully picks on His kids, the bully is going to have to deal with Him!

"When I cry out to You, then my enemies will turn back. This I know, because God is for me" (Psalm 56:9).

"If God is for us, who can be against us?" (Romans 8:31).

Remember, the battle is the Lord's—not ours. Even so, we have our jobs to do, in His strength, as His servants. One of those jobs is to exercise our authority and confess Him out loud so the adversary can hear it.

# THINK ABOUT IT—TALK ABOUT IT

## C: Confess the Lord

Are pagan gods real?

---

Should we be concerned about pagan curses?

---

What does it mean to confess the Lord?

---

Why is it important to confess the Lord with your mouth?

---

How should we fight the shield bearers?

---

What should you say to a giant?

---

How does the enemy defy the Lord when he comes against us?

---

According to verse 47, what were God's people to learn from Goliath's defeat?

---

# THE GOLIATH CODE

G:    Geography—Understand the Geography

O:    Opponent—Recognize Your Opponent

L:    Labels—Use the Right Labels

I:    Intrepid—Be Intrepid

A:    Aim—Aim to Please God

T:    Truth—Speak the Truth

H:    Hardware—Use the Right Hardware

C:    Confess—Confess the Lord

O:    Overcome—Overcome!

D:    Demonstrate—Demonstrate Your Faith

E:    Endure—Endure to the End

# Part III

# THEY DID NOT LOVE THEIR LIVES UNTO DEATH

# Chapter Nine

# OVERCOME

## HISTORY: THE ATTACK

"So it was, when the Philistine arose and came and drew near to meet David, that David hurried and ran toward the army to meet the Philistine. Then David put his hand in his bag and took out a stone; and he slung it and struck the Philistine in his forehead, so that the stone sank into his forehead, and he fell on his face to the earth. So David prevailed over the Philistine with a sling and a stone, and struck the Philistine and killed him" (1 Samuel 17:48-50).

The time for talking was over. David put his feet where his faith was as he charged straight at the enemy. On David's part there was no marching or simply drawing near. He ran straight toward Goliath. When everyone else in the Lord's army ran away from the battle, David ran to it.

Notice the Bible says he hurried and ran. He didn't even stop to pray. Why? He was already "prayed up." Even a cursory reading of the Psalms proves David was a man of prayer who spent hours alone with God. His relationship with God was one of continual, unceasing prayer. I have no doubt he carried on a conversation with God while running.

"Be merciful to me, O Lord, for I cry to You all day long" (Psalm 86:3).

"Pray without ceasing" (1 Thessalonians 5:17).

As he ran, David reached into his bag, took out a stone, loaded it in his sling, whirled it around and around and released it with expert timing. The stone struck Goliath right under his helmet, in what was probably the only vulnerable spot on him.

According to ChristianAnswers.net, a sling can propel a stone at least 60 miles per hour. An expert like David could probably sling much faster than that. His stone hit the giant with so much force, it actually shattered the giant's skull and buried itself into his forehead.

Goliath fell face down into the dirt.

Notice that David never once called the giant by his name.

Why had the shield bearer not blocked the stone with the shield? Perhaps he was too short, but even at six feet tall, he would only have been able to raise the shield as high as about eight feet. Since Goliath was nine feet nine inches tall, his forehead was probably about nine feet three inches off the ground. Therefore, David had a target area of twelve to fifteen inches above the shield and below Goliath's helmet. David's shot went over the head of the shield bearer.

What happened to the shield bearer? The Bible never mentions him again. Goliath fell forward … maybe he fell on him!

# STRATEGY: OVERCOME!

One of the most powerful labels God gives us in Christ is "Overcomer." To overcome simply means to rise over whatever comes against us.

> "Who is he who overcomes the world, but he who believes that Jesus is the Son of God?" (1 John 5:5).

When I first started speaking on this subject, I titled my notes for this section, "Run to the Battle!" In this story, that phrase seemed to encapsulate the image of David's courage, confidence, bravery, and boldness (i.e., faith). After all, most of us act more like the rest of the army. When faced with threatening giants, we often try to avoid the fight, wait for someone else to fight for us—or at least tell us what to do—or maybe even run away.

Later, I realized that charging the enemy is not always the appropriate spiritual tactic, even though it certainly was in this instance.

There are three battle tactics for a Christian warrior:

1. Charge
2. Stand (hold your ground)
3. Retreat

Scripture commands each of these. The problem is we often choose the wrong tactic for the situation at hand. Let's look at each.

## Charge

> "Therefore submit to God. *Resist* the devil and he will flee from you" (James 4:7). [Emphasis mine.]

"*Resist* him, steadfast in the faith, knowing that the same sufferings are experienced by your brotherhood in the world" (1 Peter 5:9). [Emphasis mine.]

In both these passages resist is an active verb, as opposed to passive resistance.

"I will *run* the course of Your commandments, for You shall enlarge my heart" (Psalm 119:32). [Emphasis mine.]

"*Go* therefore and make disciples of all the nations, baptizing them in the name of the Father and of the Son and of the Holy Spirit" (Matthew 28:19). [Emphasis mine.]

"Not that I have already attained, or am already perfected; but I *press on,* that I may lay hold of that for which Christ Jesus has also laid hold of me. Brethren, I do not count myself to have apprehended; but one thing I do, forgetting those things which are behind and reaching *forward* to those things which are ahead, I *press toward* the goal for the prize of the upward call of God in Christ Jesus" (Philippians 3:12-14). [Emphasis mine.]

## Stand

"Put on the whole armor of God, that you may be able to *stand* against the wiles of the devil" (Ephesians 6:11). [Emphasis mine.]

"Therefore take up the whole armor of God, that you may be able to *withstand* in the evil day, and having done all, to *stand*" (Ephesians 6:13). [Emphasis mine.]

"*Stand* firm therefore ..." (Ephesians 6:14). [Emphasis mine.]

## Retreat

"*Flee* sexual immorality" (1 Corinthians 6:18). [Emphasis mine.]

"But you, O man of God, *flee* these things and pursue righteousness, godliness, faith, love, patience, gentleness" (1 Timothy 6:11). [Emphasis mine.]

"*Flee* also youthful lusts" (2 Timothy 2:22). [Emphasis mine.]

"No temptation has overtaken you except such as is common to man; but God is faithful, who will not allow you to be tempted beyond what you are able, but with the temptation will also make the way of *escape*, that you may be able to bear it" (1 Corinthians 10:13). [Emphasis mine.]

All three of these tactics are suggested in one of my favorite verses:

"But those who wait on the Lord shall renew their strength; They shall mount up with wings like eagles, they shall run and not be weary, they shall walk and not faint" (Isaiah 40:31).

When the Bible talks about eagles' wings, it is most often to illustrate escape (see Exodus 19:4b and Revelation 12:14). Running here implies going forward, as in charging, rather than running away. And to walk means the same as to stand. Have you ever watched the soldiers standing guard at the Tomb of the Unknowns in Washington, D.C.? They walk back and forth, ever vigilant. Walking or standing also implies fellowship and abiding in Christ.

How can we know when to stand, retreat, or charge? The answer depends on where you are, versus where you are supposed to be.

If you *are* where you *are* supposed to be, then stand firm—hold your ground.

If you *are* where you *are not* supposed to be, then bug out. Retreat. Flee. Watch for the way of escape and the eagle's wings!

If you *are not* where you *are* supposed to be, then charge. Run. How do we know which way to run? Run to the Lord. How do we know where He is? Run to His promises in His Word.

~~~

Almost exactly seven years of self-employment and full-time teaching ministry abruptly and unexpectedly ended for me in the summer of 2008. The board of directors at the ministry where I was teaching asked me to meet with them. They each thanked me for building a solid foundation for the ministry and said they had decided to "go a different direction." I had been replaced. I had sensed for several weeks that changes were coming, but I was still shocked when it happened because we were seeing such incredible spiritual success and growth. I had never heard anything but praise for what the men were learning and becoming in Christ.

Numbed, I told Jennie, "I'm not a teacher anymore." I felt like God had suddenly revoked His calling from me; that is, until I remembered He would never do that.

"For the gifts and the calling of God are irrevocable"
(Romans 11:29).

I had no doubt that my spiritual gift was teaching and that the Lord
had called me specifically to teach. He had vividly confirmed it too
many times. I had been where I was supposed to be, but suddenly I
was not. Now where would I go?

A few weeks later, I was on my way to Texarkana for an interview
with an engineering firm. I needed a job, and they needed someone
with my experience who had a professional engineering license. But
I was really concerned about going back into secular work and felt
like I was abandoning my calling. Over and over I silently prayed a
verse I had memorized:

"You are my rock and my fortress; therefore, for Your name's
sake, lead me and guide me" (Psalm 31:3).

Jennie was driving while I reviewed my resume and prayed about
the interview. I had interviewed many prospective employees previously in my engineering career, but I had not been interviewed as
an engineer in more than twenty-eight years. I was not comfortable
with the thought of glorifying myself and my qualifications. Then
I felt led to read a chapter in Psalms. I had long ago developed a
plan to read one each day, but I hadn't yet read the one for that day,
which was Psalm 108.

"O God, my heart is steadfast; I will sing and give praise,
*even with my glory*" (Psalm 108:1). [Emphasis mine.]

*Selah.* (Whoa!)

God had just shown me how to interview by boldly giving Him praise, even while talking up my qualifications, all of which were gifts from Him.

Suddenly, my cell phone rang. It was the recruiter who had set up the interview, just checking to see how I was doing. He asked me, "Are you ready for the weird questions? Like, 'If you could be a tree, what kind of tree would you be?'" At that moment, I coined a new term: "Psalm Tree." I wanted to be like the one described in Psalm 1:

> "He shall be like a tree planted by the rivers of water, that brings forth its fruit in its season, whose leaf also shall not wither; and whatever he does shall prosper" (Psalm 1:3).

After we hung up, I read the rest of Psalm 108. Verses 10 and 11 strangely seemed as if they were spiritually highlighted.

> "Who will bring me into the strong city? Who will lead me to Edom? Is it not You, O God, who cast us off?" (Psalm 108:10-11a).

I read them to Jennie and told her I felt these verses were somehow significant to us, but I didn't understand why. We were not going to Edom: we were driving to Texarkana. I knew that the Hebrew word *Edom* means "red," but that didn't make sense to me.

The interview went quite smoothly. Nobody asked me about trees. They offered the job on the spot.

Meanwhile, Jennie went with a realtor to look at houses and found "the one." She loved it. When I asked where it was, she said *Red Springs,* a little community by the town of *Red Water.*

*Selah!*

And just to the west was the *Red River* military base—a "strong city." We made an offer that day.

The next day when my sister-in-law, who also lived in Texarkana, learned about the house and how God confirmed His leading through the Bible, she jokingly said, "Well, I won't believe it unless the name of the street is in today's Psalm." I asked Jennie what street it was on. She said, "Shadow Drive." Well, I opened my Bible to Psalm 109, that day's Psalm, and the verse at the very top of the right-hand column was:

> "I am gone out like a *shadow* when it lengthens" (Psalm 109:23). [Emphasis mine.]

Two months after we moved to Shadow Drive by Red Water, the church we were visiting drafted me to teach an adult Sunday School class. Later I was also responsible for teaching the Wednesday night Bible study. I used much of the same material I had taught at the addiction ministry, and God prospered and blessed us with many new eternal friends and family. Some of them helped me with this book, as I used an early version of it in a Bible study.

For an overcomer, obstacles become opportunities.

～

First-century believers would have used the Greek word *petros* to describe the stone that killed Goliath. Notice how Jesus uses this in Matthew 16.

"He said to them, 'But who do you say that I am?' Simon Peter answered and said, 'You are the Christ, the Son of the living God.' Jesus answered and said to him, 'Blessed are you, Simon Bar-Jonah, for flesh and blood has not revealed this to you, but My Father who is in heaven. And I also say to you that you are Peter, and on this rock I will build My church, and the gates of Hades shall not prevail against it. And I will give you the keys of the kingdom of heaven, and whatever you bind on earth will be bound in heaven, and whatever you loose on earth will be loosed in heaven'" (Matthew 16:15-19)

Because of Simon's testimony, Jesus gave him the new name *Petros* (Peter), which means a small stone. Jesus went on to say He would build His church on the *petra*, which means a "massive rock" foundation. Notice He says the gates of hell will not prevail against the church. He does not say the gates of the church are to withstand hell. The image is one of the church (the army of God) storming or charging the gates of hell's fortress. The words "bind" and "bound" also remind us of the Hebrew word *goliath*, which you recall means "bondage." In addition, the Greek word for loose literally means to break, destroy, or dissolve.

"This is the word of the Lord to Zerubbabel: 'Not by might nor by power, but by My Spirit,' says the Lord of hosts" (Zechariah 4:6).

Remember, if you are in Christ, "You're an Overcomer!" And you can be a "Psalm Tree!"

# THINK ABOUT IT—TALK ABOUT IT

**O: Overcome!**

Who is an "Overcomer"?

_____

When should we charge (run) to the battle?

_____

Describe a time when you were supposed to charge.

_____

When should we stay put (stand our ground)?

_____

Describe a time when you were supposed to stand firm?

_____

When should we retreat (bug out)?

_____

Describe a time when you were supposed to retreat?

_____

Where should we run to when we charge or retreat?

_____

What does it mean to "overcome?

_____

# THE GOLIATH CODE

G:     Geography—Understand the Geography

O:     Opponent—Recognize Your Opponent

L:     Labels—Use the Right Labels

I:     Intrepid—Be Intrepid

A:     Aim—Aim to Please God

T:     Truth—Speak the Truth

H:     Hardware—Use the Right Hardware

C:     Confess—Confess the Lord

O:     Overcome—Overcome!

D:     Demonstrate—Demonstrate Your Faith

E:     Endure—Endure to the End

# Chapter Ten

# DEMONSTRATE

## HISTORY: THE COUP DE GRÂCE

"But there was no sword in the hand of David. Therefore David ran and stood over the Philistine, took his sword and drew it out of its sheath and killed him, and cut off his head with it. And when the Philistines saw that their champion was dead, they fled. Now the men of Israel and Judah arose and shouted, and pursued the Philistines as far as the entrance of the valley and to the gates of Ekron. And the wounded of the Philistines fell along the road to Shaaraim, even as far as Gath and Ekron.

Then the children of Israel returned from chasing the Philistines, and they plundered their tents. And David took the head of the Philistine and brought it to Jerusalem, but he put his armor in his tent" (1 Samuel 17:50-54).

Children's books usually end the story at verse fifty, where David defeats Goliath with a sling and a stone. The rest of the story is not as family-friendly, though just as true and significant.

War is not a kid's game or a game at all. It is our world's ugly reality, a horrific consequence of humanity's fallen nature.

David knew that fighting Goliath was no game. The Philistines had invaded Israel to kill, destroy, and enslave God's people, and had done so with ever-increasing success since the days of Joshua. If given the chance, they would do it again.

How many times did David kill Goliath? Do verses fifty and fifty-one contradict each other? Did the stone kill Goliath or was it the sword?

The text actually says they both did. Some commentators have tried to reconcile this by saying that the stone merely knocked the giant down so David could kill him with the sword. However, a close look at the Hebrew text clearly shows that the word translated "killed" in verse fifty means killed. Transliterated as *uimetheu*, the Hebrew word literally means "put to death." The root of that word is *meth*, which means death. I used to tell the guys at the Ministry that "meth equals death." David mortally wounded (killed) Goliath with the stone from his sling.

Although Strong's Concordance assigns the same number H4191 to the Hebrew word for "killed" in verse fifty-one, there is a subtle difference in the spelling. Instead of *uimetheu*, this word is *uimttheu*. The Hebrew letter *yod*, transliterated as "e" in *meth*, has been replaced by a second letter *tav*, which in English is written as a "t."

I believe this is extremely noteworthy. In Hebrew, the letter *yod* means "hand" and implies "might" or "power." *Tav* means "mark" or "seal."

The word for "killed" in verse fifty-one means "marked or sealed in death."

Goliath had already been killed, and God's Word says so in the first part of verse fifty. His power and might had been destroyed. So why did David need to cut off his head?

I can think of at least three reasons.

First, in verse forty-six, he had publicly declared to Goliath that he was going to strike him and take his head from him. Therefore, he was simply following up on his promise. In essence, he was fulfilling his prophetic word.

Second, David needed to know for sure that Goliath was dead. Remember all those made-for-TV movies where the villain (usually a deranged ex-lover or some other monster) chases the hero or heroine until they somehow manage to "kill" the evil one in self-defense?

What always happens next? The hero drops the gun, turns away from the monster, and makes a phone call. Then the villian gets back up and shoots the hero in the back! David was not about to make that mistake. He sealed the giant's death with the sword.

Third, we know from our study above that Goliath had been killed. However, the only thing the spectators on either side knew was that he had fallen down. They may have been too far away to see the stone that felled him. Imagine the breathless hush sweeping through the Philistine ranks as everyone watched Goliath fall. No one knew what to make of it. Perhaps Goliath had only tripped and would soon get back up, putting an end to this nonsense fight.

David had to prove to the spectators that the giant was slain. The best way to do that was to stand over the Goliath and dramatically cut off his head, marking the death for all to see.

Though David did not have a physical sword in his hand, he had the Sword of the Spirit—the Word of God in his mouth and in his heart. So, David used Goliath's own sword. It must have been an incomparable weapon, as David would later say, "There is none other like it." (1 Samuel 21:9)

When the enemy soldiers realized their champion was dead, they were utterly discouraged and scurried home as fast as they could. Interestingly, the word translated "champion" here is *gibbor*. It is not the same as the earlier word for champion, which means "one who goes between two armies." *Gibbor* means "powerful bully" or "tyrant." The bully was dead, causing his minions to scatter like scared mice.

Finally, God's army woke up from their stupor. They suddenly did what they were supposed to do—fight the enemy.

They were trained, armed, equipped, and commissioned; yet, for forty days they had only drilled, discussed, and grown discouraged.

"But thanks be to God, who gives us the victory through our Lord Jesus Christ" (1 Corinthians 15:57).

They chased the enemy along the road to *Shaaraim* all the way to the gates of *Ekron*. *Ekron* means "extinction." *Shaaraim* means "double gates." I wonder how history would have been different if they had chased them all the way to extinction, rather than just to the gates. Sadly, this was not the last of Israel's trouble with the Philistines.

~

Notice verse fifty-four. This is a difficult passage that skeptics use to "prove" this story was made up. It says David took Goliath's head to Jerusalem.

Understand that there was no Jerusalem at this time. In Abraham's day, it had been known as *Salem*, which means "peace."

At the time of Saul and David, it was called *Jebus*, meaning "trample, thresh, or downtrodden." It was an unconquered, fortified city in the middle of the Israelite's Promised Land and home to the stubborn Jebusites. David was not welcome there.

According to Jewish tradition, he stuck Goliath's head on a pole and set it on a hill overlooking the gentile city, demonstrating his faith that God would someday give the city to him. He wanted to discourage its inhabitants by proving God's victory over this gargantuan enemy.

That hill became known as the place of Goliath's skull. The Hebrew word for skull is *gol*, so the hill was called *Gol-Golith*. In Aramaic, it became *Golgotha*, which we know as Calvary.

The city eventually became *Yireh-Shalem* (Jerusalem), which means, "He will provide peace."

Calvary vividly demonstrates the ultimate victory of Jesus the "Son of David" over the enemy of man and God's promise to the downtrodden that He will provide peace.

> "These things I have spoken to you that in Me you may have peace. In the world you will have tribulation; but be of good cheer, I have overcome the world" (John 16:33).

The city of Jerusalem reminds us of His promise regarding His return.

> "And Jerusalem will be trampled (*jebus*) by Gentiles until the times of the Gentiles are fulfilled" (Luke 21:24).

# STRATEGY: DEMONSTRATE YOUR FAITH

When I started on this book, I thought this section's key word should be "dead," as in, "Make sure the giant is dead." However, after discussing the chapter with my small group from church, I realized dead is not the main point of this part of the story.

According to Ephesians 6:12, we are at war with Satan's forces of darkness, whether we want to be or not, whether we like it or not, and even whether we know it or not. We cannot peacefully coexist with the giants, if for no other reason than they will not let us. According to Jesus in John 10:10, they have come to steal, kill, and destroy. This is a spiritual war—not a game. It is more real, more serious, and infinitely more deadly than any physical war.

By the way, what actually killed the giant? A little stone? A sword? According to Hebrews 11:32-34, David's faith killed the giant. That is the same weapon we overcomers must use.

> "For whatever is born of God overcomes the world. And this is the victory that has overcome the world—our faith" (1 John 5:4).

We must use spiritual weapons to fight this war. Only the Sword of the Spirit and the Word of God wielded with faith can slay the giants. No sword made for cutting flesh can kill a spiritual giant, nor can it kill a dead one. The giant of bondage dies only when we overcome him by the blood of the Lamb and by the word of our testimony. Dead is dead and no work we do can add to or take away from that.

But giants are never alone. There are hosts of wickedness watching and taunting us in our fight. More importantly, there are flesh and blood people—enslaved under their dark influence—who need to be won over to the power of God. Our words of faith alone may not be enough to convince them of our victory and cause the demons to turn tail and run. They may not even hear the words, but they will see our actions.

"Show me your faith without your works, and I will show you my faith by my works" (James 2:18).

We cannot be satisfied with quietly killing one giant and then going back to keeping sheep in obscurity. Complete victory requires us to run and stand over the dead giant and make sure everyone around us knows it is dead. How do we do that?

Of course, it depends on what giant you are dealing with. And remember, people are not giants. They may be shield busters or shield bearers, but not giants. If your giant is debt, then cutting up your credit cards is one way of cutting off the giant's head. Burning a mortgage after paying it off is another. Standing in front of a crowd and giving a public testimony of what God has done for you is also a great way to discourage the enemy.

Each Thursday afternoon at John 3:16 Ministries the men practiced what we called "Sword Drills." They memorized the books of the Bible, as well as scores of key Scriptures. They learned to find any verse anywhere in the Bible—in ten seconds or less—*before* Bible apps like YouVersion.

Why? To get them comfortable and familiar with the Bible, occupy their minds and time with the study of God's Word, and give them a sense of accomplishment, which many had never felt. It was also to hide God's word in their hearts – and demonstrate what they were learning.

They could have no visitors for their first thirty days at the ministry. When family and friends were finally able to visit at the Sunday worship service, they were always astounded to see the men turn the pages of their Bibles directly to whichever verse the preacher cited. The wonderment on the families' faces was priceless as they realized these were not the same men they had dropped off.

Perhaps the best example is water baptism, after the giant of your old sin nature is put to death upon receiving Jesus Christ as Savior and confessing Him as Lord (see "Annex 1: The ABCs of Salvation" at the end of the book for a simple description of God's plan for our salvation).

"For you died, and your life is now hidden with Christ in God" (Colossians 3:3).

"I have been crucified with Christ; it is no longer I who live, but Christ lives in me; and the life which I now live in the flesh I live by faith in the Son of God, who loved me and gave Himself for me" (Galatians 2:20).

Jesus instantly delivers you from all bondage the moment you are born again.

"Therefore, if the Son makes you free, you shall be free indeed" (John 8:36).

Also, the Holy Spirit re-creates you into a new being.

> "Therefore, if anyone is in Christ, he is a new creation; old things have passed away; behold, all things have become new" (2 Corinthians 5:17).

Nevertheless, others may not fully perceive what happened on the inside of you. Therefore, Jesus commanded baptism as a vivid, public, outward, physical illustration to mark what has already happened spiritually on the inside. The old giant of your former, sinful self is already dead and buried, but others around you may first recognize that at your baptism.

The next time you watch a baptism, imagine the spiritual hosts of wickedness fleeing in terror when they see another powerful bully is dead.

~~~

The same actions that discourage our enemies also encourage and energize the saints. Oftentimes others are more than eager to join in the battle—after seeing our faith demonstrated. Isn't that a big part of our purpose on earth anyway?

> "Let us consider one another in order to stir up love and good works, not forsaking the assembling of ourselves together, as is the manner of some, but exhorting one another" (Hebrews 10:24-25).

> "But exhort one another daily, while it is called 'Today,' lest any of you be hardened through the deceitfulness of sin" (Hebrews 3:13).

"… strengthening the souls of the disciples, exhorting them to continue in the faith" (Acts 14:22).

"… being examples to the flock" (1 Peter 5:3).

"Let no one despise your youth, but be an example to the believers in word, in conduct, in love, in spirit, in faith, in purity" (1 Timothy 4:12).

"Let your light so shine before men, that they may see your good works and glorify your Father in heaven" (Matthew 5:16).

# THINK ABOUT IT—TALK ABOUT IT

### D: Demonstrate Your Faith

What killed the giant?

_____

Why did David cut off the giant's head?

_____

What are some ways you can demonstrate your faith?

_____

Why is it important to show your faith?

_____

Who benefits when we demonstrate our faith?

_____

How does demonstrating our faith encourage other believers?

_____

How does demonstrating our faith discourage the forces of darkness?

_____

What things become new when you become a Christian?

_____

# THE GOLIATH CODE

G:    Geography—Understand the Geography

O:    Opponent—Recognize Your Opponent

L:    Labels—Use the Right Labels

I:    Intrepid—Be Intrepid

A:    Aim—Aim to Please God

T:    Truth—Speak the Truth

H:    Hardware—Use the Right Hardware

C:    Confess—Confess the Lord

O:    Overcome—Overcome!

D:    Demonstrate—Demonstrate Your Faith

E:    Endure—Endure to the End

# Chapter Eleven

# ENDURE

## HISTORY: POST-BATTLE DE-BRIEFING

"When Saul saw David going out against the Philistine, he said to Abner, 'Abner, whose son is this youth?' And Abner said, 'As your soul lives, O king, I do not know.' So the king said, 'Inquire whose son this young man is.' Then, as David returned from the slaughter of the Philistine, Abner took him before Saul with the head of the Philistine in his hand. And Saul said to him, 'Whose son are you, young man?' So David answered, 'I am the son of your servant Jesse the Bethlehemite'" (1 Samuel 17:55-58).

This graphic and rather confusing end of the story begins with a flashback that gives us a glimpse inside Saul's headquarters after David left to fight the giant. Skeptics point to this passage as more proof the story was a poorly edited fable, charging that it does not flow with the rest of First Samuel. After all, how could Saul not know who David was? He had known David was Jesse's son for some time before this battle. The previous chapter of First Samuel tells us:

> "But the Spirit of the Lord departed from Saul, and a distressing spirit from the Lord troubled him … Therefore Saul sent messengers to Jesse, and said, 'Send me your son David, who is with the sheep.' So David came to Saul and stood before him. And he loved him greatly, and he became his armor bearer.

> "Then Saul sent to Jesse, saying, 'Please let David stand before me, for he has found favor in my sight.' And so it was, whenever a distressing spirit from God was upon Saul, that David would take a harp and play it with his hand. Then Saul would become refreshed and well, and the distressing spirit would depart from him" (1 Samuel 16:21-23).

David was his personal musician and armor bearer!

Saul was not questioning who David was. He was confused about David's lineage. I have even heard some commentators use Saul's question to imply that David was an illegitimate son, but Scripture clearly says,

> "Now David was the son of that Ephrathite of Bethlehem Judah, whose name was Jesse, and who had eight sons (1 Samuel 17:12)."

Saul just could not accept that someone with David's courage and valor could have come from such common stock as Jesse. The name "Jesse" simply means "existing." There was nothing extraordinary about Jesse, other than the fact that he had eight sons (and two daughters), according to 1 Samuel 17:12. *Ephrathite* means "fruit-ful."

There was nothing in David's heritage to indicate greatness. In their condescending arrogance, Saul and Abner fell for the pagan, evolutionary lie that greatness is inherited, rejecting the truth that all men are created equal.

After David's victory, Saul and Abner were not encouraged like the rest of the army. Instead, they were envious, which becomes painfully obvious in the rest of the story seen in chapter eighteen and beyond. Envy is a work of the flesh, according to Galatians 5:21.

Saul was looking for a carnal (fleshly) explanation for David's attitude and actions. Since the Spirit had left him, he did not recognize the Spirit in David as the source of David's power.

"The Spirit Himself bears witness with our spirit" (Romans 8:16).

"The things of the Spirit are spiritually discerned" (1 Corinthians 2:14).

"Where envy and self-seeking exist, confusion and every evil thing are there" (James 3:16).

What about Abner? His name means "Father of Light." Maybe he fancied himself to be "enlightened," while God—not Abner—is the Father of Light, according to James 1:17.

Abner did not recognize the Light any more than Saul did. There is no indication he or Saul led the army in chasing the Philistines.

They had become mockers – scoffing at God's work, acting according to their own ungodly lusts.

> "These (mockers) are sensual persons, who cause divisions, not having the Spirit" (Jude 1:19).

True to form, Abner later caused the division of Israel in a civil war against David (see 2 Samuel 2).

This conversation between Abner and Saul in the king's tent is only the beginning of Saul's persecution of David. Like the religious authorities' accusations of Jesus a thousand years later, Saul and Abner insulted David by insinuating he was illegitimate.

The battle was over, but the Philistines did not honor Goliath's promise to become the Israelite's servants. The war would grind on for many more years before they would finally be subdued. David would endure years of waiting, persecution, and hardship, beginning in Saul's palace and then as a fugitive in the wilderness and enemy territory—all before receiving his crown.

# STRATEGY: ENDURE TO THE END

After big battles we tend to lay our armor aside. A major victory results in letting our guard down, forgetting that the hardest times often follow our greatest victories. That can be a costly mistake, as several biblical characters learned the hard way.

Joseph's own brothers sold him into slavery soon after he received his dreams from God about his future.

Immediately after he called down fire from heaven on Mount Carmel and shamed the pagan prophets of the demons Baal and Asherah, Elijah ran to hide in the wilderness. There, he became so depressed he wanted to die.

King Saul's disobedience to God, which ultimately resulted in the loss of his kingdom, came after his greatest victory over the Amalekites.

We Christians must always be alert. Satan never stops, so God commands:

> "Be sober, be vigilant; because your adversary the devil walks about like a roaring lion, seeking whom he may devour" (1 Peter 5:8).

Most of our time is not spent fighting big, exciting battles, but in working, waiting, and walking through this evil and fallen world. That is why the Bible is replete with commands for us to endure, stand firm, and persevere; as well as those that tell us to be steadfast, immovable, vigilant, patient, long-suffering, and strong.

A slow leak will destroy a house just as surely as a flood. And stress can kill a person as surely as a battle - it just takes longer.

"For you have need of endurance ..." (Hebrews 10:36).

Possibly the most maligned and persecuted president in the history of the United States said this about enduring:

> "If I give you one message to hold in your hearts today, it's this: Never ever give up. There'll be times in your life you'll wanna quit, you'll wanna go home. Just. Never. Quit. I've seen so many brilliant people—they gave up in life. They were totally brilliant. They were the top of their class. They were the best students; they were the best of everything. They gave up. I've seen others who really didn't have that talent or that ability, and they're among the most successful people today in the world. Because they never quit, and they never gave up. So just remember that. Never stop fighting for what you believe in and for the people who care about you." Donald J. Trump

What must we endure? Notice the words I emphasized in the verses below.

> "But you be watchful in all things, endure *affliction*, do the work of an evangelist, fulfill your ministry." (2 Timothy 4:5)

> "Yes, and all who desire to live godly in Christ Jesus will suffer *persecution*." (2 Timothy 3:12)

"You therefore must endure *hardship* as a good soldier of Jesus Christ." (2 Timothy 2:3)

"But recall the former days in which, after you were illuminated, you endured a *great struggle* with sufferings" (Hebrews 10:32-35).

"Blessed is the man who endures *temptation;* for when he has been approved, he will receive the crown of life which the Lord has promised to those who love Him" (James 1:12).

"My brethren, take the prophets, who spoke in the name of the Lord, as an example of *suffering* and patience. Indeed, we count them blessed who endure" (James 5:10-11).

"Therefore we also, since we are surrounded by so great a cloud of witnesses, let us lay aside every weight, and the sin which so easily ensnares us, and let us run with endurance the *race* that is set before us" (Hebrews 12:1).

"If you endure *chastening,* God deals with you as sons" (Hebrews 12:7).

"Therefore I endure *all things* for the sake of the elect, that they also may obtain salvation which is in Christ Jesus with eternal glory" (2 Timothy 2:10).

The biblical list includes affliction, persecution, hardship, struggle, temptation, suffering, the race, chastening, and all things.

How long do we have to endure all these things? According to James, it's until the Lord comes for us.

"Therefore be patient, brethren, until the coming of the Lord" (James 5:7).

I don't know about you, but I can't hold out that long on my own, or without all my armor.

Why do we have to endure all these things? Why is it, as Steven Curtis Chapman's song says, such "a long way home?" The Bible gives us several good reasons. We must endure so that:

we learn patience and wisdom ... (James 1:3-5)
we can be counted as blessed ... (James 5:11)
we learn obedience ... (Hebrews 8:9, 12:7)
we will receive the promise ... (Hebrews 10:36)
we can reign with the Lord ... (2 Timothy 2:12)
we can receive the crown of life ... (James 1:12)
we will not be overly exalted ... (2 Corinthians 12:7-10)
God can build our character ... (Romans 5:3-4)
and others may obtain salvation ... (2 Timothy 2:10)

As soldiers, we must learn to be more concerned about God's Kingdom and our character than about our comfort. David found peace in the pasture but we learn wisdom in the wilderness. And God refines character in the crucible.

Thankfully, God's Word also explains *how* we can endure all these things.

"But God is faithful, who will not allow you to be tempted more than you can endure, but will, with the temptation, provide a way of escape that you may be able to bear it" (1 Corinthians 10:31).

First, we must keep our armor on. Spiritual armor is not just for use in battle. God built it for endurance, so we can stand firm and be more than conquerors.

> "Put on the whole armor of God, that you may be able to stand against the wiles of the Devil. Therefore take up the whole armor of God, that you may be able to withstand in the evil day, and having done all, to stand. Stand therefore" (Ephesians 6:11, 13, 14).

I like to visualize spiritual armor as being more like Iron Man's suit, rather than the heavy armor worn by knights and soldiers. Not only does it protect us from the blows of the enemy, but it also gives us super-human strength!

Endurance depends on attitude as well as armor. Spiritual endurance requires faith (confidence), hope, love, and joy.

> "Therefore do not cast away your confidence, which has great reward. For you have need of endurance, so that after you have done the will of God, you may receive the promise" (Hebrews 10:35-36).

And what is the will of God?

> "Rejoice always, pray without ceasing, in everything give thanks; for this is the will of God in Christ Jesus for you" (1 Thessalonians 5:16-18).

To keep our attitudes right, we need to keep our eyes on Jesus. Remember what happened to Peter in Matthew 14:30 when he was walking on the water and took his eyes of the Lord? He began to sink.

"Therefore we also, since we are surrounded by so great a cloud of witnesses, let us lay aside every weight, and the sin which so easily ensnares us, and let us run with endurance the race that is set before us, looking unto Jesus, the author and finisher of our faith, who for the joy that was set before Him endured the cross, despising the shame, and has sat down at the right hand of the throne of God. For *consider Him* who endured such hostility from sinners against Himself, lest you become weary and discouraged in your souls" (Hebrews 12:1-3). [Emphasis mine.]

"These things I have spoken to you that in Me you may have peace. In the world you will have tribulation; but be of good cheer, I have overcome the world" (John 16:33).

"For to this you were called, because Christ also suffered for us, leaving us an example, that you should follow His steps" (1 Peter 2:21).

## Faith

Remember that biblical faith is confidence in the Lord and His Word. We can build confidence by getting to know the Lord and learning what His Word says about Him.

The Bible describes the Lord's endurance in detail. Here are a few instances:

"... the Lord shall endure forever ..." (Psalm 9:7)

"You, O Lord, shall endure forever ..." (Psalm 102:12)

"His seed shall endure forever ..." (Psalm 89:36)

"His truth endures to all generations …" (Psalm 100:5)

"… the truth of the Lord endures forever …" (Psalm 117:2)

"His righteousness endures forever …" (Psalm 111:3)

"Your faithfulness endures to all generations …" (Psalm 119:90)

"Your dominion endures throughout all generations …" (Psalm 145:13)

"… the goodness of the Lord endures continually …" (Psalm 52:1)

"Your name, O Lord, endures forever, Your fame, O Lord, throughout all generations …" (Psalm 135:13)

"The entirety of Your Word is truth, and every one of Your righteous judgments endures forever …" (Psalm 119:160)

"… the Word of the Lord endures forever …" (1 Peter 1:25)

"His mercy endures forever …" (Psalm 118) (repeated 5 times)

"His mercy endures forever …" (Psalm 136) (repeated 26 times)

The phrase "His mercy endures forever" appears forty-one times in the Bible. Thirty-one of those are in Psalm 118 and Psalm 136. Remember when I said forty is the number for testing and preparation? Think about this: His mercy (or grace or love or loving kindness, depending on the translation) endures forever times forty—plus one more forever for good measure!

## Hope

Although we in Christ will endure forever and His goodness endures forever, the bad things we must endure will not. When we reach our eternal home, we will fully enjoy all His promises.

"I have hope in God ... that there will be a resurrection of the dead" (Acts 24:15)

"Be of good courage, and He shall strengthen your heart, all you who hope in the Lord" (Psalm 31:24)

"Why are you cast down, o my soul? And why are you disquieted in me? Hope in God; For I shall yet praise Him, the help of my countenance and my God" (Psalm 42:11)

"I wait for the Lord, my soul waits, and in His Word I do hope" (Psalm 130:5)

"If we hope for what we do not see, we eagerly wait for it with perseverance" (Romans 8:25)

"But let us who are of the day be sober, putting on the breastplate of faith and love, and as a helmet the hope of salvation" (1 Thessalonians 5:8)

The battles and stressors we endure in this lifetime do not prepare us for retirement; they prepare us for the resurrection—and for eternity.

Pastor and author Randy Alcorn illustrates this kind of hope in one of his novels. He writes about an old deacon who was sitting on his front porch one afternoon. He was blind, crippled, and hard-ofhearing. When his pastor stopped by to visit and asked him how he was doing, he replied, "Pastor, there ain't nothing wrong with me a good resurrection wouldn't cure!" That's biblical hope!

## Love

As God's children and followers, everything we do must be done with love.

"Watch, stand fast in the faith, be brave, be strong. Let all that you do be done with love" (1 Corinthians 16:13-14)

"But I say to you, love your enemies, bless those who curse you, do good to those who hate you, and pray for those who spitefully use you and persecute you" (Matthew 5:44)

David's own name reminds us of this truth. Remember "David" means "loving." In First Corinthians, we learn that love is long-suffering, endures all things, and never fails. Furthermore, John tells us God *is* love.

## Joy

Finally, with Jesus as our example, we can endure all these things with joy.

"My brethren, count it all joy when you fall into various trials" (James 1:2).

"Rejoice in the Lord always, again I say, 'Rejoice'" (Philippians 4:4).

The word "rejoice" reminds me of the word "refuel." To rejoice simply means to refill your joy tank.

"The joy of the Lord is your strength" (Nehemiah 8:10).

"Sing praise to the Lord, you saints of His, and give thanks at the remembrance of His holy name. For His anger is but for a moment, His favor is for life; weeping may endure for a night, but joy comes in the morning!" (Psalm 30:4-5).

Paul reminds us:

"And He said to me, 'My grace is sufficient for you, for My strength is made perfect in weakness.' Therefore, *most gladly* I will rather boast in my infirmities, that the power of Christ may rest upon me. Therefore, I *take pleasure* in infirmities, in reproaches, in needs, in persecutions, in distresses, for Christ's sake. For when I am weak, then I am strong" (2 Corinthians 12:9-10). [Emphasis mine.]

In the Orthodox Jewish Translation of the New Testament (which is included in the free YouVersion Bible app), the Hebrew word for "grace" in 2 Corinthians 12:9 is *chesed*. This is the same word translated as "mercy," "love," or "loving kindness" in the phrase "His mercy endures forever." The Hebrew word for "strong" in 12:10 is *gibbor*, which is one of the words translated as "giant" elsewhere.

In other words, Paul tells us God's never-ending grace, mercy and love are sufficient for us; and when we are weak, then *we* are giants!

Never, ever, give up.

# THINK ABOUT IT—TALK ABOUT IT

## E: Endure to the End

Why is the phrase, "all men are created equal" incompatible with paganism and evolution?

_____

Why were Saul and Abner not encouraged by David's victory?

_____

Why do we tend to take our armor off after a victory?

_____

List some things we must endure:

What do we gain by endurance?

_____

How can you endure?

_____

Keep your _____ on.

Keep your _____ right. Spiritual endurance requires _____, _____, _____, and _____.

Keep your eyes on _____.

To "rejoice" means to _____ your _____ tank.

# THE GOLIATH CODE

G:    Geography—Understand the Geography

O:    Opponent—Recognize Your Opponent

L:    Labels—Use the Right Labels

I:    Intrepid—Be Intrepid

A:    Aim—Aim to Please God

T:    Truth—Speak the Truth

H:    Hardware—Use the Right Hardware

C:    Confess—Confess the Lord

O:    Overcome—Overcome!

D:    Demonstrate—Demonstrate Your Faith

E:    Endure—Endure to the End

# EPILOGUE

David's victory vividly illustrates how we too can conquer our giants. I created the mnemonic "GOLIATH CODE" to help you remember and apply David's story to yours.

Whenever you face a giant, remember:

**G: Geography—Understand the Geography.** Your enemy is wedged between a hedge and a fence and can never cross the boundary of the blood. You, on the other hand, are in Christ the Ram—the position of strength.

**O: Opponent—Recognize your Opponent.** Learn to recognize spiritual giants and the bondage they bring. Don't waste your time or ammunition fighting the shield bearers.

**L: Labels—Use the Right Labels.** Never accept the labels Satan or the world tries to stick on you. You are who God says you are, not what you do.

**I: Intrepid—Be Intrepid.** Do not fear. Don't be afraid. Have confidence in God and in His Word.

**A: Aim—Aim to Please God.** Keep your focus on the mission and the Audience of One. Ignore distractions. Silence the distracting shield busters by answering their questions with questions.

**T: Truth—Speak the Truth.** Counter the lies told by the deceiving shield busters with the truth of God's Word and your own testimony.

**H: Hardware—Use the Right Hardware.** Put on the whole armor of God, every day. Only spiritual armor is completely effective in spiritual warfare. And all our battles are spiritual.

**C: Confess—Confess the Lord.** Speak the Word. Call out Jesus' name. If you belong to God, say so. Say it aloud. Use the authority you have as a Child of the King.

**O: Overcome—Overcome!** If you are in Christ, you're an overcomer. Learn when to charge, stand your ground, or retreat.

**D: Demonstrate—Demonstrate your Faith.** Discourage the enemy and encourage the family of God by showing them your faith by your works.

**E: Endure—Endure to the End.** Memorable battles come and go, but keep your armor on until you hear the Lord say, "Come up here!" Practice faith, hope, and love with joy. We are not home yet, but I've read the end of the Book—we win!

In the meantime, we get to wear armor more awesome than Iron Man's!

# Annex 1

# THE ABCS OF SALVATION

What must you do to become a new creation and receive eternal life?

Admit you are a sinner.

> "For all have sinned and fall short of the glory of God" (Romans 3:23).

You cannot be good enough or do well enough to earn your way into God's perfect heaven.

> "For the wages of sin is death, but the gift of God is eternal life in Christ Jesus our Lord" (Romans 6:23).

We have all earned the judgment of eternal death, which is separation from God, but God offers us the gift of eternal life "in Christ." It is free to us, but Jesus paid for it with His own blood. He earned the title "Lord".

**B**elieve Jesus is who He says He is.

> "For God so loved the world that He gave his only begotten Son, that whoever believes in Him should not perish, but have everlasting life" (John 3:16).

Jesus is God's first-born Son. If you believe in Him, you'll not suffer the wages of sin and *will* have life forever.

> "Most assuredly I say to you, he who believes in Me has everlasting life" (John 6:47).

You can be sure that the moment you believe in Him, you have everlasting life. You don't have to wait until death to receive it.

**C**onfess Jesus as your Lord.

> "That if you confess with your mouth the Lord Jesus, and believe in your heart that God has raised Him from the dead, you will be saved. For with the heart one believes unto righteousness, and with the mouth confession is made unto salvation" (Romans 10:9-10).

This is not confession of sin. You already did that when you admitted it. To confess something with your mouth is to say it aloud. "Lord" means owner (as in landlord), boss, or master. Rather than your lord being you, say that Jesus is your Lord.

Jesus' resurrection proved that the sacrifice of His sinless life was accepted by God as the complete payment for all our sin debt. To "believe in" means to trust your life to Him.

"Therefore whoever confesses Me before men, him I will also confess before My Father in heaven. But whoever denies Me before men, him I will also deny before My Father who is in heaven" (Matthew 10:32-33).

When you tell others about Jesus, He tells God the Father about you!

"For whoever calls on the name of the Lord shall be saved" (Romans 10:13).

Good news! No matter who you are or what you've done, once you call on Jesus' name as explained above, you become a new creation and the gift of eternal life is yours. God's Holy Spirit places you "in Christ" and actually sets up residence in you.

God no longer labels you as "ungodly" or "sinner." You are "righteous" and a "saint." Now go act like it!

# Annex 2

# HEBREW NAMES

Abinadab: Father of Liberals

Azekah: Fence

Bethlehem: House of Bread

David: Loving

Ekron: Extinction or Eradication

Elah: Strength, God

Eliab: The God of Our Fathers

Elyon: Most High

Ephes-Dammim: Boundary of the Blood Drops

Ephrathite: Fruitful

Goliath: To place in bondage, send into exile. Also: Splendid

Gath: Winepress

Israel: Prevailing with God

Jebus: To thresh, trample

Jerusalem: City of Peace, God will provide peace

Jesse: Existing

Philistine: Rolling or migrating

Saul: Demanding

Shaaraim: Double gates

Shammah: Stunned or Stupefied

Sochoh: Hedge

# Annex 3

# WHO WE ARE IN CHRIST

A Chosen Generation (1 Peter 2:9)

A Dwelling Place of God In the Spirit (Ephesians 2:22)

A Holy Nation (1 Peter 2:9)

A Royal Priesthood (1 Peter 2:9)

Able To Do All Things Through Christ (Philippians 4:13)

Abraham's Seed (Galatians 3:29)

Accepted in the Beloved (Ephesians 1:6)

Adopted (Romans 8:15)

Alive Together with Him (Colossians 2:13)

Already Clean (John 15:3)

Ambassadors for Christ (2 Corinthians 5:20)

Appointed to Affliction (1 Thessalonians 3:3)

Authorized (Luke 10:19)

Baptized By One Spirit into One Body (1 Corinthians 12:13)

Becoming the Righteousness of God (2 Corinthians 5:21)

Being Transformed into His Image From Glory To Glory (2 Corinthians 3:18)

Believers (Acts 5:14)

Beloved of God (Romans 1:7; Colossians 3:12)

Blameless (Colossians 1:22; 1 Corinthians 1:8; 1 Thessalonians 5:23; Psalm 37:37; Proverbs 2:21; 11:5; Philippians 3:6; Luke 1:6)

Blessed With Every Spiritual Blessing (Ephesians 1:3)

Born Again (1 Peter 1:23)

Born of God (1 John 5:1)

Bought at a Price (1 Corinthians 6:20)

Bound To Thank God Always (2 Thessalonians 1:3; 2:13)

Brethren (Matthew 23:8)

Called (2 Thessalonians 2:14)

Called by His Name (Acts 15:17)

Called Into the Fellowship of His Son (1 Corinthians 1:9)

Children of God (John 1:12; 1 John 3:1)

Children of the Promise (Galatians 4:28)

Chosen (Revelation 17:14)

Chosen Generation (1 Peter 2:9)

Christ's (1 Corinthians 3:23)

Clay in the Potter's Hand (Isaiah 64:8)

Clean (John 13:10)

Complete (Colossians 2:10)

Created in Christ Jesus for Good Works (Ephesians 2:10)

Crucified with Christ (Galatians 2:20)

Debtors, but Not to the Flesh (Romans 8:12)

Delivered from the Power of Darkness (Colossians 1:13)

Dependent on the Lord (Isaiah 10:20)

Dwelling Place of God in the Spirit (Ephesians 2:22)

Empowered (2 Timothy 1:7)

Epistles of Christ (2 Corinthians 3:3)

Escaped From the Corruption That is in the World (2 Peter 1:4)

Family (Ephesians 3:15)

Followers of the Lord (1 Thessalonians 1:6)

Forgiven of all My Trespasses (Colossians 2:13)

Free Indeed (John 8:36)

Gifted (Romans 12:6)

God's Building (1 Corinthians 3:9)

God's Fellow Workers (1 Corinthians 3:9)

God's Field (1 Corinthians 3:9)

Granted To Suffer (Philippians 1:29)

Hard-Pressed On Every Side, Yet Not Crushed (2 Corinthians 4:8)

Healed (Isaiah 53:5)

Heirs According to the Promise (Galatians 3:29)

Heirs of God (Romans 8:17)

His Disciples (John 8:31; 13:35)

His Friends (John 15:14)

His Own (John 13:1)

His Own Special People (1 Peter 2:9)

His People (Psalm 100:3)

His Sheep (John 10:27)

His Workmanship (Ephesians 2:10)

Holy (1 Corinthians 3:16-17; Colossians 3:12)

In Christ Jesus (1 Corinthians 1:30)

In God (Colossians 3:3)

In Him Who is True (1 John 5:20)

Indwelt (Romans 8:11)

Joint Heirs With Christ (Romans 8:17)

Just (Hebrews 10:38)

Justified (1 Corinthians 6:11)

Kings (Revelation 1:6)

Light In the Lord (Ephesians 5:8)

Little Children (1 John 2:1; Galatians 4:19)

Living Stones (1 Peter 2:5)

Loved (1 John 4:10)

Loved by God (Galatians 2:20)

Members of His Body (Ephesians 5:30)

Members of One Another (Ephesians 4:25)

Members of the Household of God (Ephesians 2:19)

Ministers of the New Covenant (2 Corinthians 3:6)

More Than Conquerors Through Him (Romans 8:37)

New Creations (2 Corinthians 5:17)

New Lumps (1 Corinthians 5:7)

No Longer Slaves (Galatians 4:7)

No Longer Strangers and Foreigners, but Fellow Citizens with the Saints (Ephesians 2:19)

Not in the Flesh but in the Spirit (Romans 8:9)

Not of the World (John 15:19)

Not Our Own (1 Corinthians 6:19)

Not Under Law but Under Grace (Romans 6:14; Galatians 5:18)

Of God (1 John 5:19)

Of the Truth (1 John 3:19)

Of Those Who Believe (Hebrews 10:39)

One in Christ Jesus (Galatians 3:28)

Overcomers (1 John 4:4)

Partakers of Christ (Hebrews 3:14)

Partakers of Grace (Philippians 1:7)

Partakers of His Promise in Christ (Ephesians 3:6)

Partakers of the Heavenly Calling (Hebrews 3:1)

Partakers of the Holy Spirit (Hebrews 6:4)

Partakers of the Inheritance of the Saints in the Light (Colossians 1:12)

Partakers of the Sufferings (of Christ) (2 Corinthians 1:7)

Perplexed, but Not In Despair (2 Corinthians 4:8)

Persecuted, but Not Forsaken (2 Corinthians 4:9)

Precious (Isaiah 43:4)

Predestined to be Conformed to the Image of His Son (Romans 8:29)

Priests (Revelation 1:6)

Receiving A Kingdom Which Cannot Be Shaken (Hebrews 12:28)

Reconciled (Colossians 1:21)

Redeemed (Galatians 4:5; Psalm 107:2)

Righteous (Romans 5:19; 9:30; 1 Peter 3:12; Philippians 3:9; Psalm 1:6; 32:11; 37:19&39; Luke 1:6)

Safe (Proverbs 18:10)

Saints (Romans 1:7)

Sanctified (1 Corinthians 6:11)

Saved (1 Corinthians 15:2)

Saved by Grace (Ephesians 2:8)

Sealed (2 Corinthians 1:22; Ephesians 1:13; 4:30)

Servants of Christ (1 Corinthians 4:1)

Serving the Lord Christ (Colossians 3:24)

Set Free From Sin (Romans 6:18)

Slaves of God (Romans 6:22)

Slaves of Righteousness (Romans 6:18)

Soldiers of Jesus Christ (2 Timothy 2:3)

Sons of God (Galatians 3:26; Galatians 4:6)

Sons of Light (1 Thessalonians 5:5)

Sons of the Day (1 Thessalonians 5:5)

Stewards of the Mysteries of God (1 Corinthians 4:1)

Struck Down, but Not Destroyed (2 Corinthians 4:9)

Subject To Christ (Ephesians 5:24)

Sufficient (With Our Sufficiency From God) (2 Corinthians 3:5)

Surrounded By a Great Cloud of Witnesses (Hebrews 12:1)

The Apple of His Eye (Zechariah 2:8)

The Body of Christ (1 Corinthians 12:27)

The Branches (John 15:5)

The Elect of God (Colossians 3:12)

The Fragrance of Christ (2 Corinthians 2:15)

The Light of the World (Matthew 5:14)

The Lord's (Romans 14:8)

The People of His Pasture (Psalm 95:7)

The Salt of the Earth (Matthew 5:13)

The Sheep of His Hand (Psalm 95:7)

The Sheep of His Pasture (Psalm 100:3)

The Temple of God (1 Corinthians 3:16)

The Temple of the Holy Spirit (1 Corinthians 6:19)

The Work of His Hand (Isaiah 64:8)

Triumphant (2 Corinthians 2:14)

Truly Unleavened (1 Corinthians 5:7)

Unable to Do Anything Without Him (John 15:5)

Upright (Psalm 32:11; 37:18; Proverbs 2:21; 29:10)

Valuable (Matthew 10:31; Luke 12:7)

Victorious (1 Corinthians 15:57)

Washed (1 Corinthians 6:11)

Witnesses (1 Thessalonians 2:10)

# ABOUT THE AUTHOR

**BLAKE WATKINS** is a licensed Professional Engineer and licensed minister. After earning his Master of Science degree in Engineering, he worked as an electrical engineer and as a supervisor of engineering, information technology, and process control teams for a global Fortune 100 chemical company. He and his wife Jennie also owned and operated a Christian bookstore called The Lamb's Way. He served as an ordained deacon, a Gideon speaker, and a pulpit-supply preacher. In his spare time, he traveled and taught biblical worldviews and creation science, using a scale model he built of Noah's ark.

After twenty-one years in engineering, he answered God's call to full-time ministry, took early retirement, and concentrated on his speaking and teaching ministry. During that time, he created and taught a comprehensive life-application curriculum based on the armor of God in Ephesians 6, for a very effective addiction ministry.

After seven years of ministry, he returned to full-time engineering and relocated to Texarkana, Texas, where he taught adult Bible studies two to three times each week. He now lives in Sand Springs,

Oklahoma, working as Principal Electrical Engineer for a major natural gas company. He teaches Sunday School and a live, weekly, online Bible study.

Together Blake and Jennie have taught children's Sunday School, led successful young adult and adult Sunday School, and also evening Bible studies. They were the founding leaders of a 4-H club in their hometown of Batesville, Arkansas. Married since 1978, they are blessed to be parents and grandparents.

www.ingramcontent.com/pod-product-compliance
Lightning Source LLC
Chambersburg PA
CBHW071737120626
46550CB00002B/555